FENG SHUI
AND THE
5-ELEMENT KITCHEN

FENG SHUI
AND THE
5-ELEMENT KITCHEN

Ilse Maria Fahrnow, M.D.
Jürgen Heinrich Fahrnow
Günther Sator

Table of Contents

Foreword

According to the Chinese philosophy of Taoism, the five elements of wood, fire, earth, metal, and water represent everything that exists in nature—from the four seasons to the food we eat. Furthermore, everything is caught up in a process of change. Thus, one element strengthens another or originates from it (fire, for example, is nourished by wood). This basic principle is the foundation of the two wisdom teachings of Feng Shui and Five-Element Cooking.

By now, we modern Westerners also acknowledge that our food does much more than merely supply us with calories and nutrients. For beyond what is measurable, everything that surrounds us is full of something invisible, something that interconnects all things: energy. You absorb from your food primarily "energy vibrations," and only secondarily nutrients. Even the furniture, colors, and utensils in your kitchen—everything from the dining table to the table decorations—all that has an energetic impact on your well-being. The many tips in this book demonstrate how you can increase your vitality with simple means. First use Feng Shui principles to create a cheerful, stress-free, communicative atmosphere in your kitchen, for the good mood of the cook is carried over into the food he or she prepares. Then, if the eating area also has a friendly, positive energetic vibration, every meal can become a festival of the senses and a healing force. Almost without realizing it, you will activate life energy for yourself, your family, and your guests. We wish you much pleasure and enjoyment.

Günther Sator

Living in Harmony

Surely you too have experienced how in some living spaces your life force feels especially charged with energy and full of inspiration, whereas in others, after only a short time, your "energy battery" feels dead. Why is it that you feel so good in some places, whereas you experience others as unpleasant or even irritating?

The Power of Energy in Your Home

MANY people are investing more and more money, energy, and time in their private living spaces. It's easy to see why: They can feel just how important a harmonious living environment is for their personal well-being. Thus, there is a noticeable trend toward giving careful thought to one's personal living space. Experts say that the power of energy in the home is the most important untapped potential of our day. And so, it's no surprise that more and more people are beginning to design their living spaces with awareness, as an antidote to stress and increasing pressure at work. But home decorating and design should not only be about creating a pleasing visual effect. It is also an energetic process.

HOW you arrange your home is no coincidence. Your personality and your current life situation express themselves in your living space and its furnishings. Thus, for example, the design and arrangement of your kitchen and dining area say a lot about your family life and the character traits, strengths, and weaknesses of the people who are part of it. In other words, your home can reveal much more about you than you might have ever thought possible. And likewise, conscious design of living spaces can have numerous favorable effects on one's life. On the following pages you can learn how to optimally design your kitchen and dining area, and where to pay special attention in furnishing your kitchen, while cooking, and in your day-to-day life in the kitchen area.

Your Home — Your Lifestyle

THERE is a deep connection between your home environment and the many, seemingly unrelated experiences of everyday life – your work, your friendships, your relationship, and your health. And, incidentally, having a beautiful or luxurious living space is not really the issue here. On the contrary: Sometimes it is precisely the elaborately furnished homes that lack a feeling of inner harmony.

"Panta rhei" – "Everything flows," said the ancient Greeks. In other words, everything changes.

Everything is Energy

BEHIND everything that surrounds us there is a hidden force. According to the old teachings, everything in our universe is made up of an energy that is invisible, but which permeates everything. This vital force is everywhere: in the landscape, in buildings, and inside living spaces. This global energy irradiates and influences the environment and shapes human life. This is why people develop differently in different environments. But this invisible energy also is responsible for the fact that everything changes and evolves, and nothing will be the same tomorrow as it was yesterday or is today. Even if the speed of change is usually too slow for us always to be able to recognize it at once, nonetheless, everything strives for change. No relationship remains unchanged; every tree, every blossom, every space, every person, every fate— everything changes. This transformation happens according to certain laws. Basically it represents the continuous effort of nature to change and grow. Herein lies a powerful opportunity, for the process of transformation is based on clear principles. If you understand these and apply them correctly in everyday life, your life will become increasingly harmonious. For then you will be in harmony with the laws of nature.

More Pleasure out of Life

THUS a balanced lifestyle and a harmonious, energy-charged home are the key to a successful and happy life. Then you will be able to connect the inner (your life, your personality) with the outer (your environment). Feng Shui brings these two aspects into alignment and helps you to achieve a greater understanding of life. It reveals the connections between things and helps remove obstacles. As a result, you get more pleasure out of life, enjoy better health, greater success, and more surprising and enriching experiences.

The natural flow of energies can be seen, for example, in the change of the seasons.

We Are Shaped by Our Surroundings

EVEN science now recognizes that we are affected by the environment in which we live. Everything is energy, everything is full of vibrations, everything is "alive"—the descriptions are many and varied, but they help us to understand why we feel especially good in some places, and not in others. Or why some people make us feel good, while in the presence of others we feel weak or even depleted.

ALL this has to do with energy—with your own, and with the energy of things, which also means the energy of your surroundings. Personal

A harmonious design of the space within your own four walls can have a positive effect on your life.

resonance determines whether a room, a piece of furniture, a color, a person, or thing makes you feel good or does you harm. Not only landscapes and places radiate energy; everything does, and thus everything influences and affects everything else. Also, every man-made object, whether it's a cupboard, a picture, a cup, a table, or even a freshly prepared dish straight from the oven, is ultimately a carrier and expression of this universal energy.

Chi

THE only question is, what are the properties of this energy, or "chi" (also known as *qi*, the Chinese word for vital energy)? Just as a heavily trafficked road radiates a different energy compared with a colorful spring meadow, some objects, furniture, shapes, colors, or foods can contain either enhancing or draining, weakening chi.

FENG SHUI, the ancient Chinese teaching of harmonious living, offers a wealth of tools and tips which can help you to enhance the quality of your home and, thus, the quality of your life. And enhance them you should! For in our increasingly stressful and demanding lives, it becomes more and more important to have a home that enhances and harmonizes one's vital energies.

The Importance of the Kitchen

Your home is a cohesive organism in which a variety of different tasks and functions need to be integrated in a harmonious fashion. Accordingly, not only the placement of the individual rooms in relation to one another is important, but also their harmonious furnishing and arrangement.

THE art is to make the best possible use of the potential inherent in the environment, but also to design the interiors in such a manner that they "produce" the best possible chi for their inhabitants. Feng Shui is the art of implementing the right measures in the right place at the right time. Measures that create a general feeling of well-being lead to a healthy and successful life. Disturbances should be avoided. The ideal is for all rooms of the home to be designed and utilized so well that the vital energy chi can flow freely and without disturbance. Each room is important for the overall energy structure. Any Feng Shui deficiencies should be compensated for with suitable measures (see tools and tips on page 28). And in this, the kitchen plays a vital role.

A Place for Communication

FIRST of all, the kitchen symbolizes health and energy – the foundations for a harmonious life. In the course of a kitchen's life, many thousands of meals are prepared there. Each of these meals can either have a positive or a detrimental effect, depending on the ingredients and mode of preparation. On the other hand, a well-utilized kitchen can also become an important communication center for both family and guests.

Balm for any relationship: a relaxed conversation in the kitchen or at the dining table

11

AS a rule, conversations go better in a pleasant, nourishing, and fragrant atmosphere than in a more sober place.

SURVEYS have shown that families who lack this central place of the kitchen in their daily life experience more marital problems, and that these problems are more difficult to resolve than those who have a pleasant kitchen environment. Thus, the kitchen also takes on an important role as mediator in relationships. When this connecting function is lacking, it often needs to be laboriously worked out in some other area.

BUT even for singles, regular and joyful use of the kitchen is important. It is here that your self-love is mirrored, that is, how much you pay attention to your own desires and needs (both acknowledged and hidden). You should pamper yourself just as you would pamper your guests!

Harmonizing Your Kitchen

FOR all the above-mentioned reasons, your kitchen should have as functional and harmonious a design as possible, so that feelings of comfort, harmony, strength, and happiness can be generated here. The person who does the cooking should be absolutely protected from any disturbing influences, so as to create a propitious environment for him or her and his or her family and guests. This has a direct and positive affect on the food prepared in such a kitchen and its quality.

Energy Wants to Flow

THE kitchen was always considered the healing space, the apothecary of the home. "Let your food be your medicine," admonished the wise men of Asia centuries ago. For the harmony of food carries over directly to the people who eat it. Nonetheless, good ingredients alone do not make for good food. Several different components need to harmonize so that good ingredients can be turned into energy-charged, vitalized food.

Energy and Health

ANY naturopathic physician knows that health is only possible when the body is well provided with energy. Thus, blockages—of any kind—need to be dissolved. One example of how this knowledge has been applied for centuries is the Chinese art of acupuncture. It teaches that the human body has so-called "meridians," or energy channels, located on or just beneath the skin. When energy is blocked in one of these meridians, a fine needle is inserted into it. This dissolves the blockage, and the chi can flow freely once again—a prerequisite for healing. Inside the home, Feng Shui guidelines bring stagnated energies back into flow; thus Feng Shui can be thought of as acupuncture for rooms.

How does Feng Shui Work?

IN a living system, everything is connected with everything else. Just as in our bodies, the dissolving of blockages in one area can precipitate healing in seemingly unrelated areas. In the same manner, the conscious activating of individual areas in a home can harmonize the whole.

EVERYTHING in our environment is "alive," and so we can easily imagine that, like our bodies, our home needs to be provided with a good energy supply. The vital force chi should circulate through the rooms like a couple dancing the waltz. Would that be possible in your home without any obstacles? Is the entrance to your kitchen quite hidden, and is the dining area hard to access? If so, you should do something about these blockages!

Feng Shui for the West

HERE in the West, Chinese methods are often simply taken over without asking whether they make sense for our lives. Of course the fundamental laws that govern our world are the same in China, the motherland of Feng Shui, as in the West. But many rules that are too "Chinese," or in other words, which reflect regional peculiarities or superstitions, should be omitted, and in their place new, independent methods more suitable for the West should be applied.

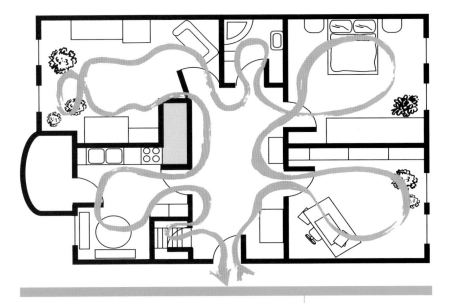

THIS means that Feng Shui for the 21st century should be developed in part to suit our Western culture. Don't worry—you can forget about bamboo flutes and you don't need to remodel your kitchen to look like a Chinese restaurant. After all, our own culture has developed enough Feng Shui tools of its own. And since nowadays we are confronted with new situations, new solutions are required. Today there are many modern methods that correspond to Western tastes that are available to us. Good Feng Shui is, above all, attractive and aesthetic. Let yourself be surprised at how varied and universally applicable the resources of our own Western culture can be.

The energy should flow through your home like a couple dancing the waltz.

Chi and the Kitchen

The more harmonious the kitchen, the more energy-charged and healing the food prepared in it will be.

ABOVE all else, food should be as free as possible of chemicals and other toxic substances so that the body does not lose energy unnecessarily. For this reason, natural ingredients from organic farms are ideal. The second component is a series of energetic measures that help us absorb the chi from our food. The most important are good air (Feng) and energy-charged water (Shui). These two elements are vitally necessary for life on earth.

Good Feng—Good Air

THE air we breathe is responsible for 90 percent of our metabolic processes. Fresh air has strong chi and provides us with positive energy, while stale or stagnant air weakens the body or even makes it sick. To regenerate oneself, one should make sure to take deep breaths of fresh air on a regular basis. In Japan and some parts of the U.S., there are already "oxygen bars" for this purpose.

Make Your Kitchen a Haven of Good Feng

● Make sure your kitchen has good ventilation and adequate air circulation. Kitchens need windows! Both gas and electric ranges produce air pollution through the burning of dust and other particles. While ventilator hoods improve the air quality, they have other negative side effects, since they draw chi out of the kitchen.
● For optimal burning and the lowest possible level of air pollution, gas ranges should burn with a blue flame.
● Healthy, strong houseplants purify the air in the kitchen. For example, spider plants, peace lilies, or gerbera daisies are good for this purpose.

Regular airing and green plants ensure good Feng—good air— in the kitchen.

Energizing Shui— Drinking Water

THE other vital element of our life is our drinking water. It should be charged with energy (for this there are now many methods) and, above all, it should not be stored in plastic bottles. For proof of the negative effects of plastic bottles, you can conduct a simple experiment: Put a plastic bottle filled with water in the sun for a few hours. You will notice how the taste changes. This is because plastic discharges particles into water.

Enemies of Chi

● Chlorinated water attacks Vitamin E, and even though it evaporates, it produces toxic organic substances that do not evaporate.

● Avoid accumulating aluminum in the body (associated with Alzheimer's and other diseases of the nervous system) by not using aluminum pans or foils. Teflon and other nonstick surfaces are also toxic. When overheated, they can generate dangerous vapors.

● The best things to use are glass containers or good ceramic dishes for serving—they're also good for storing leftover food.

Chi in Food

THE other component of Feng Shui has to do with the energy or chi of cooking and eating. Even the way in which you cut something affects the quality of the food. You may have noticed that a bite from an apple tastes different from a cut slice. Sometimes children insist on having their lunch sandwich cut in a particular way. And often a cook will intentionally choose a particular shape of noodle, even though all of them are made out of the same dough.

What Affects Food?

● A smooth, clean cut with a sharp knife charges food with clarity and precision, while a dull blade transmits hard, rough energy to the food.

● "Love goes through the stomach": If you are in a good mood while you are cooking, or, especially, in love, or even just happy, the food you prepare will be of better quality and also taste better. Even the mood of everyone sitting at the table will be noticeably improved.

● As we have all experienced, the consciousness of the cook can also affect the quality of the meal. If for no other reason, home-baked bread or Grandma's pies taste so good simply because they were made with love.

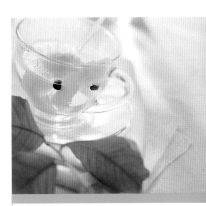

Also important: vital water—"living Shui"

Many restaurants offer at best "fillers" instead of nourishing, much less healing food. When did you last feel truly energized, light, and in good spirits after a restaurant meal?

● Have you ever thought about how it affects your meals when you have to cook under pressure or stress, or against your will, or if you aren't feeling well physically or emotionally? In such instances the energy of frustration, anger, or stress is transmitted to the food you're preparing. Stress produces more stress; the food becomes saturated with negative energies. No wonder people get into arguments so often at the dinner table.

● If you don't cook very often under stress, the effects will not be as bad. But what might the consequences be if you and your family eat such negatively charged food on a regular basis, over and over again?

Food cooked over a wood fire has the highest energetic value.

Which Stove is Best?

IN terms of undesirable energy, microwave ovens are in the same category as food preparation under stress. Though they supposedly preserve more vitamins and nutrients than other cooking methods, due to the unnatural heating process (from the inside out, as opposed to normal cooking, from the outside in) it also aggressively destroys the cell structure of food. While what you eat may be heated through and perhaps even look appetizing, energetically speaking it is toxic waste. Over time, chaos in food leads to chaos in people.

Wood Provides the Best Heat

AN experiment was conducted, comparing the properties of various energy sources. Water was brought to a boil by means of four different sources of heat: wood, gas, electricity, and microwaves. Then, plants were watered with the water after it had cooled down. The plants that grew the healthiest and strongest were those treated with the water boiled on a wood fire. The plants with the water from the gas range were also extremely healthy and almost as strong. The water from the electric range produced a bent and somewhat crooked plant. And the microwaved plant could hardly be called anything but a mutant, and it grew weaker from day to day.

THUS, wood fire provides the most vitality—which is why even the simplest food prepared over a campfire is usually more appealing and healthier than food cooked anywhere else.

IF you can't do without a microwave oven completely, you should at least use it sparingly and with discretion. Don't place the appliance over the stove or too close to where you eat—otherwise the chi that rises from your regular stove, or your own personal chi, could be unfavorably influenced.

Kitchen Appliances

IN modern kitchens we see more and more electric appliances, a fact which also results in increased pollution through electromagnetic fields—so-called "electrostress." This can drain people energetically and make them tired and susceptible to illness. For this reason, at the very least you should use regular light bulbs instead of fluorescent lights, have sufficient plants around the house, and air out rooms regularly.

APPLIANCES that come into direct contact with food, such as blenders or electric mixers, give food a rough, choppy quality. For this reason, such appliances should be used only infrequently, for over time anyone who eats too much food prepared in these fast-running machines will become restless and seem out of balance. The disharmonizing effect of such electric appliances can be lessened somewhat by letting the food rest for several minutes before serving.

As Little Technology as Possible

WHENEVER you can, you should use gentle, slow cooking methods, for this produces quieting, harmonizing qualities in food. Cooking in a pressure cooker favors focus and concentration. Pan frying stimulates active energy, and light food helps create a light spirit.

WE should never eat when we're stressed or pressed for time. Taking a short, deep breath before the meal and thankfully contacting the "spirit" and the energy of the food activates the digestive functions and makes it easier to absorb the food's vital energy.

THOROUGH chewing aids direct absorption of chi from food. Chi is absorbed through glands that lie underneath the tongue, which is why the first sip of hot soup can warm the entire body. Each type of food has its own chi. Of special value are locally produced, organic foods. Each food is attributed to one of the five elements—wood, fire, earth, metal, and water (see the tables starting on page 59)—the theory of which is also an important pillar of Feng Shui.

More energy and clarity through precision cutting: Knives should be well sharpened.

The Optimal Kitchen

The happier the cook, the more energetically charged the food. For this reason, in laying out your home you should consider very carefully which area would be the ideal space for cooking and eating.

Wind chimes can moderate an energy flow that is too strong.

IDEALLY the kitchen and dining area should be easily accessible from the living room or other frequently used rooms. Whoever is working in the kitchen shouldn't have to feel excluded, but should be included in on whatever is going on. A cozy counter with comfortable chairs invites both family members and guests to sit and chat while meals are being prepared. This creates a feeling of togetherness, especially when the kitchen is a bit out of the way. In such a kitchen people feel at ease, and no one, including the cook, feels as though they'd like to escape.

PARTITIONS between the kitchen and living areas that can be opened or closed as needed have proven very practical. A kitchen that is used frequently and with pleasure activates the chi of both the home and the persons who live there, charging it with favorable vibrations. A bleak, neglected kitchen, used—or abused—only for making coffee or wolfing down fast food, creates deficiency and stagnation, because the "bagua area" (see pages 32 and following) attributed to the kitchen is receiving too little attention and energy.

First Stop—The Kitchen

IF you can see straight from your front door into the kitchen, then cooking, eating, and enjoying food are especially important to you. Whether you tend to have problems with weight, eat out of boredom, or to compensate for stress or depression, follow a strict diet or nutritional theory, or just have an intense appreciation of gourmet delights—in one way or another, eating is an important focus of your life. Perhaps you frequently enjoy sharing meals with friends. If, however, this preoccupation with eating should start to seem exaggerated to you, you can choose among a number of Feng Shui guidelines to moderate the kitchen's strong influence.

● Divert the attention as much as possible away from the door to the kitchen or dining area, preferably toward the living room or another important room in the house. Provide a striking and attractive eye-catcher on a highly visible wall: A picture, a sculpture, a colorful bouquet of flowers, or a nice piece of furniture, well lit and displayed, can draw people's attention and also chi past the kitchen to the living room.

● Hang wind chimes, a mobile, or a rainbow crystal directly in the energy flow between the front door and the kitchen, to disperse the energy.

● Attach the object to the ceiling in such a way that the chi is channeled in the desired direction and the object itself doesn't obstruct the passageway (it helps to hang it fairly high). Lamps can also moderate and disperse chi—the clearer the illumination, the stronger the effect. You can also emphasize the desired energy direction with spotlights or rows of lights. Shine them in the direction you want the chi to flow.

● The direction in which the floor surface is laid out is also important. Tiles that are laid diagonally or crosswise moderate the flow of energy toward the kitchen area. A runner lying perpendicular to the entrance or a round rug also has a moderating effect on the room's energy.

Tips for Kitchen Design

HERE are some easy tips on how you can design your kitchen according to Feng Shui principles.

Light

A Feng Shui kitchen gives a very bright and friendly impression. Adequate daylight is especially important, but at nighttime, too, there should be sufficient lamps to create a warm and pleasing atmosphere. As a rule, most kitchens have insufficient lighting. This leads to stagnation in the room's energy flow. Often only the "important" areas around the work areas and the kitchen table are well lit. But if the lighting is poor

in the corners, over cupboards, or, even worse, over the sink or stove, or if the lamps are mounted in such a way that they shine in people's eyes, this can noticeably disturb the atmosphere for cooking and eating. Dark areas are also areas of stagnating chi, which is something to be avoided at all costs in a kitchen, or anywhere food is prepared.

To ensure light, uplifting chi, the kitchen should be designed to be bright and friendly.

Neatness

LEFTOVER food lying around for days, unwashed dishes, dirty countertops, and a crusty stove are very unfavorable, from a Feng Shui perspective. For optimum chi, the kitchen should be orderly, and it should also be cleaned. A neat, clear workplace enhances creativity and makes it easier to achieve an ideal flow of chi.

Appliances

ANOTHER important thing to make sure of is that all appliances and tools work properly. For instance, the stove represents life force and health, and also financial well-being. Anyone who eats good food feels good, and anyone who feels good usually is more fortunate in work and, as a consequence, in finances as well. Thus, the correct placement of the stove is particularly important (see page 25). It is also important, however, that you use the stove regularly. The more frequently you make active use of your resources, the better. For this reason, too, you should use all of the different burners regularly. This helps you in your daily life to activate all your talents and abilities in a more balanced manner and not to overemphasize one aspect at the expense of others. For the same reason, a stove with four or more burners offers more potential from the outset than one with fewer burners.

A dripping faucet allows energy to leak away unused.

Eliminate Disturbances

IF one of your stove's burners is not working, it can mean in a figurative sense that you are not applying part of your resources in your own life. For this reason it is important to repair anything that is broken or no longer works properly as quickly as possible. This helps you to avoid stagnation, making it easier for you to stay "in the flow." Creaking or sagging doors, drawers that stick, chipped or cracked plates or glass, an oven that doesn't work properly, a dishwasher that leaks, or a burned-out light bulb are all signs of beginning stagnation.

IF the water faucet is constantly dripping, it not only increases your water bill. In symbolic terms, a part of your life energy and your finances are leaking away unused. The vital element water (Shui) is an important carrier of healthy and vital chi and thus also a sign of abundance and affluence. If your drain is stopped up, Feng Shui experts conclude that you either have a hard time completely letting go of old, used-up things (also in a figurative sense), or that you have a tendency toward digestive problems. For all these reasons, any irregularities or disturbances in the kitchen or dining area should be eliminated and compensated for as quickly as possible. This enhances your well-being, lifts your energy and also your mood, and helps you to take better advantage of your opportunities.

Color

THE color of the kitchen should support both the people who use it and the food that is prepared there in a warm, inspiring way. Too much gray, black, or other dark colors would make the room appear unnecessarily heavy and somber. Likewise, an excess of stainless steel, chrome, and highly polished, dark stone can feel cold, serious, and sometimes even hostile to life. Good design doesn't need to feel sterile. According to the law of yin and yang (see page 23), the various elements, colors, forms, and materials should be integrated into a harmonious whole. In other words: If you would like to use a lot of dark colors, you need to be sure to also include balancing light touches. Straight lines and hard surfaces need soft, round, and flowing objects as a balance. And if there is only limited space available in the kitchen, and the room feels cramped and dark, the furnishings, color, and lighting should be particularly light, airy, and friendly.

THUS, everything has its counterpart. And if in the end the emphasis is more on friendly, light, open, and expansive aspects, you will not only feel very comfortable in this kitchen; you will also prepare food that has a positive effect on the people who eat it.

This white kitchen in a traditional style has a light, expansive feel to it. It exudes restrained elegance.

An extravagant kitchen: Color and soft, rounded forms create a flowing energy.

PROPITIOUS colors for walls are white (which symbolizes purity and clarity), as well as all light, not too bright colors. Creamy pastel tones, subtle beige, or a soft yellow create warmth and a harmonious atmosphere.

FENG SHUI warns against red in the kitchen, because it would increase the "fire" of the cooking stove, which would provoke stress and restlessness. But here, as anywhere else, the quantity is what counts. How much red you can use in your kitchen really depends on how light, how dynamic, and how yang its overall appearance is.

IF the visible surfaces of your furniture have an especially striking color, the walls and ceiling should probably remain white for balance. Extensive surfaces of dark blue (water element) are suitable for kitchen design only to a very limited extent, and if used at all should probably be combined with metal (gives a cool, restrained feel) or wood. Here, too, several houseplants or other "woody" elements would probably be a good idea, for wood mediates between the water energy of the color blue and the fire energy of the stove.

Yin and Yang in the Kitchen

THE philosophy of yin and yang describes all things or phenomena of our universe as "pairs of opposites" (yin/yang) that are in constant interchange and dialogue. Each side needs the other as a complement in order to be whole.

THE yang principle is active, while the yin principle is passive; nonetheless, nothing is exclusively one or the other, for in each thing slumbers the seed of its opposite. When the night is at its zenith (midnight, maximum yin), already the day is beginning (yang). In the deepest winter (yin) nature is already preparing for the germinating, budding, growing, and blossoming of the warm season (yang). And even the stormy period of youth (yang) transforms over the course of the years into the relatively more tranquil period of old age (yin). Anyone who works a great deal (yang), but also grants himself or herself regular and sufficient pauses for rest (yin) will remain healthy and successful over time. But anyone who lives and acts in an unbalanced manner will soon feel the harsh consequences of his or her self-induced imbalance.

YIN and yang should also be somewhat balanced within the home—though it should be noted that perfect balance is not possible, because everything is always caught up in the process of change. Thus, in the kitchen and the dining area there should be sufficient vital, inspiring, and refreshing yang chi, complemented by a lot of harmonizing yin energy, which provides comfort and atmosphere, for example in the form of curtains, rugs, tablecloths, or cozy furniture for sitting and relaxing.

YOU should avoid the extremes of a kitchen that is overly bright, hot, noisy, busy or open (yang) on the one hand, or extremely dark, low-ceilinged, crammed, or poorly ventilated (yin) on the other. In all things the middle path should be sought. This is different for each person. Aspire to that state that corresponds best to you and your family and that supports what and who you are. And if a particular design or situation no longer fits you, then all you have to do is change it by adjusting imbalances and enhancing those qualities that now correspond better to who you are.

Yang	Yin
Active	Passive
Heaven	Earth
Outside	Inside
Male	Female
Light	Dark
Time	Space
Expanding	Contracting
Extroverted	Introverted

The symbol for yin and yang: Female and male, light and dark—the one always requires the other.

A well-designed kitchen with lots of light and sufficient space is ideal.

Furniture

STRAIGHT furniture edges stimulate left-hemisphere, linear, logical brain activity, while soft, rounded, flowing forms enhance right-brain, creative energies. An ideal kitchen integrates both kinds of energy. You should avoid "cutting chi" (arrow-like energy that emanates from sharp corners) wherever people need to pass close by or right next to places where people often sit or work. The edges of countertops and prominent cupboards or storage units should be slanted or rounded off (see, for example, page 22).

THE height of work surfaces should also be carefully considered, for optimum chi can only flow through your body when your spine is held straight. For this reason you should insist on higher countertops, if your height requires them for comfort. After all, over the years you're going to be spending thousands of hours in the kitchen, and the slight extra expense will pay for itself in a very short time.

Keep the Space Clear

IF at all possible, make sure that not all your wall surfaces are covered with hanging cupboards. Having large objects in front of your head while you cook is an obstruction that hampers your creativity and detracts unnecessarily from the light, airy atmosphere you want to create in your home's kitchen.

FOR this reason, ventilator hoods should only be installed when absolutely necessary. If you're buying a new one, choose one that's small, rounded, and unobtrusive. And be sure to change or clean the filter regularly.

GENERALLY speaking, sufficient space and room to move is especially important in the kitchen. Only if you feel free and unhampered will the food you prepare also take on the vibration of freedom. So keep the work area as unobstructed as possible, and make sure you have enough surfaces for putting things on, so that when you cook you can let your creativity unfold freely.

The Placement of the Stove

SINCE food is in a state of transformation while it is being cooked, it directly absorbs the agreeable vibrations of a happy and contented cook. On the other hand, food that is prepared by a stress-filled or frustrated cook is full of destructive energy.

THE ideal position of the most important piece of kitchen equipment, the stove, is in the kitchen's "power spot." If you are designing a new kitchen, choose a central spot from where you have a good view of the room and door(s). From such a position of power, the quality of the food you prepare will be much higher. If the stove is too close to the door, the in-flowing chi might become too strong. In this case, placing a rainbow crystal or a mobile between the entrance and the stove can help to modulate the energy flow.

IF your stove happens to be in a position where you have to stand with your back to the door, or, especially, if it is in the corner of the room, you can use mirrors to get a better overview and feel more in control. If you don't want to hang a mirror behind the stove, cheery-sounding wind chimes hung by the kitchen door can serve as an acoustic guardian and protector. You will be surprised how positively your emotional state will be affected by the security you gain in this manner.

Other Kitchen Appliances

BE sure when positioning water and refrigeration elements, such as sinks, dishwashers, washing machines, refrigerators, or freezers, that you don't place them right next to the stove, since this would create a conflict between the elements fire and water. If this placement is unavoidable, at least you should install something from the wood element as a mediator between water and fire, for instance, by hanging a wooden cooking spoon or some such object right above the line of demarcation between the two conflicting elements.

A mirror behind the stove optically doubles the number of burners (as well as the amount of the food prepared), which symbolizes an increase of potential affluence.

The Dining Area

The atmosphere in a room depends a great deal on its design. Furniture and accessories, the choice of lighting and color—many things need to coordinate so that people can feel comfortable in a space.

DEPENDING on the function of the room, the object that is most important for this function should be given preferential treatment and particularly highlighted. In an office this will be the desk, in a living room, the sofa and armchairs, and in the dining room, the dining table. A good and harmonious atmosphere during meals is especially important, because even food prepared with much love and joy will lose its healing vibrations if there is a "heavy vibe" at the table.

Quarrels and arguments over dinner will spoil the most wonderful meal. If you don't already eat in the kitchen ("living room/kitchen"—usually a very propitious arrangement), the dining table should be in a brightly lit room next to the kitchen. Since people need enough room so that they don't feel closed in or trapped, the table in a small room should not be too big.

Lift Your Guests' Spirits

CREATE an atmosphere of ease in the dining room. Particularly important are a pleasing wall treatment, friendly accessories, and harmonious pictures. The more stimulating and cheerful the room's atmosphere, the better everybody's mood will be while eating. For this reason, it's better to avoid objects and motifs that are dark and somber or evoke a sense of melancholy. Remove any furniture or accessories that have a loaded history. Heirlooms, antiques or furniture belonging to an ex-partner often radiate unpleasant vibrations. Such furnishings—valuable as they may be—can be a source of constant irritation. If you can't "clear" such pieces (see page 29), then you ought to get rid of them.

Unfavorable: Toaster and microwave oven are out of place here!

The Ideal Dining Table

THE size of the table should be suited not only to the room, but also to the most frequent type of use. For example, if a three-person family gathers daily at a table that is too large, then at least you should keep the father's unfinished work files or the child's homework from piling up at the other end. It's better to place a nice candle in this spot, or fill it with a vase of fresh flowers. Otherwise the family will lose part of their inner cohesion, because foreign influences are symbolically burdening their private life. Likewise, wobbly table legs or unsteady tabletops should be repaired as quickly as possible, to keep inconstancy and instability out of your life.

Form and Material

TO ensure optimum chi in the dining room, choose a dining table with a harmonious and balanced form. Beneficial tabletops have a rectangular, square, round, oval, or octagonal shape. Triangular tables, on the other hand, or ones with an asymmetrical surface or with cut-off corners create inharmonious vibrations. For this reason, these oddly shaped tables are known in Feng Shui as "quarrel tables."

BUT not only irregularly shaped tables are considered problematic. Practical as they may be, drop-leaf and expandable tables with visible joints

Tablecloth and flowers bridge the crack between the table and the leaf.

or cracks can create "separating energies" and thus trigger subtle stress. If family members sit on different sides of the crack, its subliminal separating effect can manifest itself. For this reason, it's better to bridge the crack with a round vase and fresh flowers. Likewise, a pretty cloth placed over the crack, a bowl with fruit, or a hand-made ornament can ensure the desired harmony at the table.

TABLETOPS made of glass or Plexiglas create an unstable effect. In a sense the food appears to be almost floating in midair, and the subconscious judges this as uncertainty. Over the course of time this can affect your mood, and perhaps even your health. Ensure greater stability by using a tablecloth. Tablecloths also harmonize tables with cut-off corners.

Feng Shui Tools and Tips

There are a variety of Feng Shui tools and accessories that can help you to balance out problem areas and raise the energy in the kitchen and the dining area.

IF a door and a window are located directly across from each other in a room, an "energetic draft" results; that is, too much chi is lost through the window, and at the same time, the room is filled with a palpable sense of restlessness. You can interrupt and disperse this draft, for instance with the help of a mobile or a small- to medium-sized set of wind chimes. A healthy plant on the windowsill, ideally in combination with a hanging ornament such as a pretty mirrored ball or perhaps a shiny brass sun, can modulate the chi flow and protect the room from energy loss. At the same time, the reflecting accessories divert the energy back into the room.

Crystals, Mirrors, and Chimes

A rainbow crystal hung in front of the windowpane can also stop the energy flow and divert it back into the room. When sparkling crystals shine their brilliant colors over the dining area or the stove, this harmonizes the room's vibrations and creates a cheery, joyous atmosphere. When hung over the dining table, rainbow crystals have a quieting, harmonizing effect—but they should always be clean, and their surfaces should sparkle.

MIRRORS have a similar effect: If you have your back to the door when you stand at the stove, or if your stove is in the corner of the room, mirrors can help you to gain a better overview. Besides, a well-placed mirror optically opens the space behind the stove, which gives the entire cooking area a more airy, expansive, and also brighter feel. And since Feng Shui also attributes the symbolism of abundance and affluence to the stove, "doubling" the nourishing chi of food is supposed to have a positive effect on the family's wealth. It's certainly worth a try. However, mirrors can only display their beneficent influence when they are cleaned regularly—which, after all, is usually much easier than, say, scrubbing tiles. Shiny, metallic surfaces can also be used as a substitute for mirrors. And if you have a ventilator hood that looks very bulky, a strip of mirror on the front can make it recede visually.

IF you don't want to hang a mirror behind your stove, cheery-sounding wind chimes by the kitchen door can serve as an acoustic guardian and protector, informing you of movements behind your back. The increased sense of security will give a noticeable lift to your emotional well-being.

When sunlight falls on rainbow crystals, it magically fills the room with countless specks of light in rainbow colors.

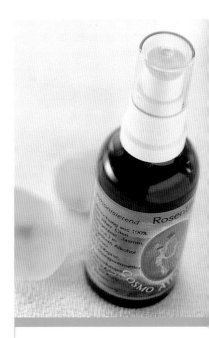

*DNA spirals increase
the room's vibrations.*

Accessories

DNA spirals are not only fascinating, they can also greatly enhance a room's vibrations—as, incidentally, can indoor fountains, or pictures with water themes. And your dining area should never be without houseplants or cut flowers, which symbolize the dynamism of new life, while improving air quality and increasing chi. You can use light to activate stagnant areas, such as unused corners–for instance, in the form of a floor lamp or spotlight. Or you can create life in such areas by hanging up an interesting mobile.

Room Cleansing with Rose Elixir

BY now you know how important clear and harmonious vibrations in a room are for a person's general well-being. But even in the most beautiful kitchen or the most harmonious dining room, over time a large amount of old energies will accumulate. Every conversation, every thought, every newspaper or news report you read here, and particularly every argument or worry, is preserved in the environment. Gradually the room's vibration is lowered. At first it is imperceptible, but after a while everything feels a little heavier or "grayer" than before. For this reason, all rooms—especially the kitchen and eating area—should be "energetically cleansed" on a regular basis. Here it should be noted that the clearer, finer, and higher the vibration of the tool you use to purify, the better the effect.

THE simplest and quickest method is to spray the room with "Feng Shui Rose Elixir." For this you need an elixir made of the finest ingredients. Add a little rosewater spray to a bucket of water and wipe off walls, furniture, and other objects with a slightly dampened cloth. After the cleansing, the atmosphere in your rooms will feel clean, like after a refreshing summer rain. Friends who know your home may ask you if it's been freshly painted, or if you've moved the furniture around.

REPEAT this cleansing about every two to three weeks. Or, even more simply: Whenever you intuitively feel like it, probably on an average of every few days, just spray a little rosewater spray in the air. Your family will thank you. The extremely high, crystal-clear vibration as well as the lovely fragrance will have a harmonious effect on all family members.

*You can buy rosewater
spray in specialty and
health food stores.*

Eating without Distractions

THERE are many different factors that decide whether or not your food's Feng Shui will ultimately be advantageous: high-quality ingredients, preferably organic, the energy in your kitchen, careful, gentle processing and preparation of food, the atmosphere in the dining area, and the way you eat your food.

EVEN the best-quality food will lose much of its chi if you read the newspaper, talk on the phone, work, or study while you eat. Can you even remember what you ate for lunch today, or for dinner yesterday? If you had to hesitate even for a moment and stop and think, your thoughts weren't focused on your meal with your full attention. "When you work, work; when you eat, eat; and when you love, love," says an old Asian proverb.

Books, newspapers, and stock reports should be taboo at the table!

ONLY a person who lives entirely in the present, in the here and now, can truly enjoy life and actively guide his or her fate. For the past is over, and the future is only just emerging–out of the now. Focus on the current moment.

Enjoyment with All the Senses

A phenomenon that science is only beginning to discover is that our food consists of far more than just its material components. The most important part is the "energetic data." These are transmitted mainly through vibrations. The foundation for this is the principle of resonance. Whenever you are attuned to "spiritual garbage" in your thoughts and feelings, the energies you attract from your environment will be of an equally low quality: Like attracts like. If, on the other hand, you attune yourself with openness and gratitude to the positive potential in a situation or a thing, you will take in with all your senses everything that is good in the environment. Even if it sounds a little corny: Your life will become a daily "miracle."

YOU can practice this attitude at least three times a day—when you eat. And you will quickly notice that not only does your whole meal taste different, but also your whole life will take a turn for the better. Everything that is inessential falls away, and many new and wonderful things come to take its place. For good Feng Shui is more than just pushing furniture around and choosing

tasteful decor—it is an attitude toward life that always aspires to make the best out of everything. And that always begins with you!

An important part of a lovingly prepared meal is a beautifully set table.

The Bagua: Where Is Your Kitchen Located?

Every spot, every room in your home has its own special energetic function. One Feng Shui tool with which you can discover the energies hidden in your own four walls is the "bagua."

The basic line (see below), where the areas Knowledge, Career, and Helpful Friends are located, corresponds to the wall where the entrance door is located.

THE bagua is a sort of mirror of your personality. It tells you about your strengths and about areas of your life that are yet to be developed. By implementing specific Feng Shui measures in the various areas, you can address those energies that will help you to develop more efficiently on your life path.

THE nine zones are descriptions of individual spheres of life. Their names are Career, Relationships, Family, Prosperity, Unity (or Tai Chi), Helpful Friends, Offspring, Knowledge, and Fame. For the purposes of wholeness, ideally all these areas should be present in the ground plan of your home (each level is treated separately), which is always the case with a rectangular or square plan.

What the Bagua Says

IF all the bagua areas are completely represented in your home, that is a good point of departure. All this really says, however, is that a relatively uniform potential is present for all the various spheres of your life. Much depends on how the individual areas are designed and utilized. A neglected or overly stuffed room in the Relationships corner, for instance, can indicate problems and encumbrances in your relationships, while a beautifully designed living room where you enjoy spending time, located in the same area, points to a harmonious and heartfelt relationship. Remember that nothing is a coincidence, and all external manifestations, including home design, are always a symbol and an indication of an inner potential.

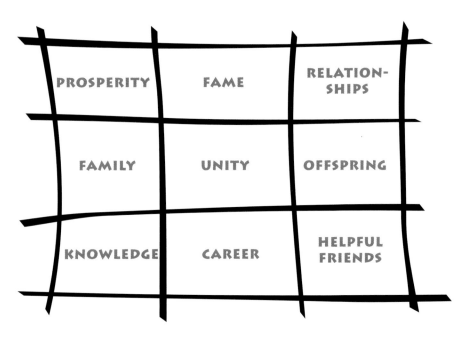

PROSPERITY	FAME	RELATION-SHIPS
FAMILY	UNITY	OFFSPRING
KNOWLEDGE	CAREER	HELPFUL FRIENDS

Ideal: the dining table in the kitchen.

The Bagua and Your Kitchen

DEPENDING on where the kitchen and the dining area are located on the bagua grid of your dwelling, it can mean something special for your kitchen. For each area has a different energy structure, and this is in turn shaped and overlaid by the strong energy of food, cooking, and eating.

The Kitchen in the Career Area

HAVE you experienced moments when your life seems to be just flowing right along? All you do is take the first step, and suddenly the most wonderful things start happening, almost by themselves? This enriching experience is closely connected with the Career area, which is located in the middle of the baseline of the bagua grid. It describes the flow of your professional and personal life. And it also reflects how well you have already succeeded in uniting your inner essence with your outer life. For this reason, this area of your home should always be free of obstruction, open, and designed in a flowing manner.

IF your kitchen or dining area is located here, there is much nurturing, nourishing chi that flows in the area of your life path—a very good omen, if kitchen and dining area are used regularly and function well. Make sure the color white predominates, and include some green, for example, in the form of a houseplant.

The Kitchen in the Relationships Area

IF you would like to improve your relationships with friends, colleagues, neighbors, and your partner, it is worth taking a closer look at the part of your home that is located in the right back corner, in relation to the entrance. For long-term enhancement of your relationships, you should

The Career area

The Relationships area

remove all broken, obstructive, disturbing objects from this area and clean the room thoroughly. In particular, any symbols representing loneliness or solitude have no place here. Much better are objects in pairs.

A well-utilized kitchen is ideal in the Relationships area, since it shows that relationship is just as important as good, regular meals. If, on the other hand, you only cook or eat here sporadically, the Relationships area will be lacking part of its energetic charge. Accordingly, from now on you should devote more attention to your relationships—and to your kitchen in the Relationships area. A little bit of red and ceramics or terra–cotta as materials are enhancing features.

The Kitchen in the Family Area

THE Family area is located in the middle of the bagua grid and on the left side. It represents your roots and ancestry, that is, everything that came before you. Since the past is the foundation for your present and future, it also gives an indication of your strengths and weaknesses in relation to your parents, your ancestors, and also your superiors. In addition, this area has much to say about your personal growth potential, which is why it should be structured as clearly as possible, and not be cluttered with junk. For this reason, clearing out old things you no longer need is a very important step.

The Family area

The Prosperity area

IF your kitchen or, particularly, your dining area is located in the Family area, you seem—at least in this particular house or apartment—to have an easy time of working through and processing your past, and you should make the most of this opportunity. The more balanced and regular the use of your kitchen and eating area, the better it will be for an autonomous and equal relationship with your parents and relatives. Your relationship with your employer or other superiors can also become more harmonious. Always keep your kitchen clean and tidy, and integrate something green (such as houseplants) or light blue into the room design.

The Kitchen in the Prosperity Area

THE bagua area of Prosperity is devoted to that which is usually called "inner riches," but also to finances and self-esteem. It is located in the left back corner, seen from the baseline. The ability to recognize a hidden opportunity and deeper meaning in everything that happens to you is also anchored here. Accordingly, this zone can tolerate a good deal of abundance and lushness.

The more varied the use you make of your kitchen, if it is located in this zone, the better—for instance, for discussing topics that are important to you and your family, for exchanging experiences with others, and for inspiring each other reciprocally. If, in addition, you also celebrate cooking and eating accordingly, the Prosperity area will be further strengthened. A half-full bowl of fresh water and pretty flowers are favorable for the bagua area of Prosperity.

The Kitchen in the Unity Area

THE center of the home, called Unity, or Tai Chi, is your energy refueling center. It can be compared with the center of the human body. For you to feel really centered, balanced, healthy, and full of strength, the Tai Chi area should be as free and open as possible—no walls, no chimneys, no storage rooms. A light, airy, warm room design is ideal for this spot.

IF the kitchen is located in the Tai Chi area, it should not be designed as a separate room, but rather as a space that is integrated into the whole. Overall, it should give a sense of lightness, like the food that is prepared here. If the dining table happens to mark the center of the home, a striking light fixture over the table or a "centering" object in the middle of the table (for instance, a vase or a bowl of fruit) can serve to stabilize the Tai Chi area. Here you should never leave the table untidy. Incorporate light yellow and some pottery or ceramics and perhaps also a crystal into your Tai Chi bagua area.

The Kitchen in the Helpful Friends Area

THE bagua area entitled Helpful Friends has to do with any form of spontaneous, voluntary, helpful support. It is located in the lower right corner of the bagua grid and is devoted to active helping and help received, to humanity in action, and, if you will, to a "Higher Power."

A well-utilized kitchen in this area indicates that you probably have a rather well-developed network of helpful friends in your life. If you also frequently use the kitchen (and the same goes for the dining room in this area) to entertain friends and guests, this will activate your personal willingness and desire to be there for others when they need you. Giving and receiving is the overarching theme of this area, and the more "nurturing gifts" you prepare in your kitchen for your family and guests, the more often you too will be able to enjoy helpful support in your life. The colors white, silver, gold, as well as yellow, orange, and brown fit in well here. Also propitious are earthy or metallic accessories such as crystals, ceramics, or wind chimes. This is also a good place for displaying little knickknacks that remind you of loved ones and friends, or that you received as gifts from them.

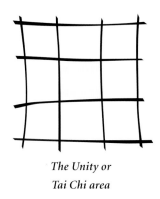

The Unity or Tai Chi area

The Helpful Friends area

The Offspring area

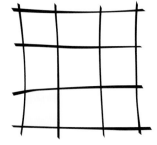

The Knowledge area

The Kitchen in the Offspring Area

ALL your physical and "spiritual" children, that is, not only your own offspring, but also anything that has to do with ideas, projects, and creativity, is at home in this area. In addition, it mirrors your potential for renewal and rejuvenation.

THUS, a kitchen in the Offspring area has an inspiring effect, and you may enjoy experimenting and surprising guests and family members with your own inventive gourmet creations. This inspiration and creativity will probably also manifest in your daily life, not only in dealing with children, but also in the form of creative ideas in your work or private life. Metal and round forms (for example, a dining table) fit in well here. Favorable colors for a kitchen in the Offspring area are off-white and soft shades of yellow.

The Kitchen in the Knowledge Area

OF all the different bagua areas, it is important for the Knowledge area to remain the quietest. It lies in the left lower corner of the bagua grid and represents your professional competence on the one hand, and that which is generally known as "inner knowledge" on the other.

HOW your kitchen is designed and utilized, if it is located in this area, shows your personal access to your inner knowledge. For example, a busy, loud, disorderly kitchen would indicate that amidst the hectic busyness of everyday life you probably only rarely find time for quiet and reflection. The "knowledge energy" gets lost. If, on the other hand, daily food preparation in the kitchen as well as enjoyment of the food prepared are treated as something special, then a great deal of propitious chi energy will flow here, which will enable more direct access to your inner voice. Above all, there should be no noisy TV set or radio here to cause shallow diversions. Instead, empty glasses and other empty containers favor the energy of the Knowledge area, as well as stone, ceramics, and a touch of red.

Favorable for the Knowledge area: empty glasses.

Cooking together is good for any relationship.

The Kitchen in the Fame Area

THE Fame area is located at the top middle of the bagua grid. Among other things, it is related to your aura, your charisma, and, as a result, also to how you are perceived and judged by others. If the energies are balanced in this area, you will be able to animate and inspire others by your mere presence and aura, and a self-confident demeanor characterizes you.

IN principle, this is a particularly auspicious spot for a kitchen. It should, however, have a balanced design that takes all five elements into account, and above all, the fire energy (for example, the color red) should not be too strongly emphasized. In addition to the usual functional furnishings, objects that radiate beauty should enhance the kitchen and dining area. Fresh flowers are a must!

Mindfulness to Enhance Chi and Increase Your Enjoyment of Life

THE more love and care you invest in your kitchen, your ingredients for food preparation, and, most importantly, yourself, the more life energy you will acquire. Talk your partner and your children into an occasional visit to an open-air market and a joint cooking spree. The more intensively each family member occupies him- or herself with shopping, cooking, and perhaps also with the designing of a harmonious inner space, the more value is attributed to food—and its energy. Anyone who shops, cooks, and eats with joy and awareness gets a lot more out of the experience in the end, for wherever consciousness and joy are present, there you also find chi. We wish you much fun, energy, and health from and with your Feng Shui cooking!

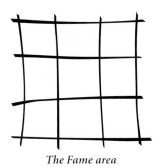

The Fame area

Each and every organism, each and every person, is made up of five elements: wood, fire, earth, metal, and water. Furthermore, each food is attributed to one (or several) of these elements. Whether after eating you feel fit and full of energy on the one hand, or empty or overstuffed on the other, depends not least on the proportions of the five elements in your meal. Since energetically sound nutrition based on the principles of five-element cooking is not only healthy but also delicious, it has quickly found many devotees. Your body will show you the way: If you feel good, your food has provided you with enough energy. If you feel cold or tired after eating, the various foodstuffs were not balanced, or they were energetically "empty."

If you prepare the recipes in the following chapters, you can supply yourself with each of the five elements and enhance the flow of your life force, chi. Your body will thank you, and your spirits will also be lifted. Human beings are composed of living energies that form a whole, and anything you add from outside benefits this whole.

This book offers you valuable, healthy nutritional recommendations, recipes that accelerate the healing process in case of illness, and generally enhance health, as well as dishes you can indulge in without worry, even if you have problems with your weight —enjoyment without regret. This is ensured by harmony in the kitchen and a balanced composition of the five elements in your diet.

Bon appétit!

Ilse Maria Fahrnow, M.D.

Jürgen Fahrnow

The Dance of the Cosmos—
Vital Energy

All forms of manifestation in the cosmos consist of light energy. This energy flows through all forms present in the visible and invisible worlds. You can feel it in your body when you are happy, relaxed, and full of *joie de vivre*. When you experience pain, your natural energy flow is blocked.

As Above, So Below—
As Inside, So Outside

SEVERAL thousand years ago, in China, the theory of energy and vitality was formulated, and for about the last 100 years scientists have been confirming the fundamentals of this model.

MAN and environment are one, says a Chinese proverb. And just as you can give your home, your kitchen, and your dining area a harmonious design based on Feng Shui principles, with the help of balanced nutrition you can increase your energy and enjoyment of life. Then outer harmony becomes inner harmony, and your body gives you the gifts of health and well-being.

The Importance of Balance

ACCORDING to Chinese thought, a human being is healthy when his or her organism possesses vital energy in abundance, which flows harmoniously in the rhythm of day and night and in the rhythm of the seasons. A deficiency of this energy creates fatigue and lethargy and over time can result in illness.

SOME people have sufficient energy, but it gets congested in certain areas of the body. Tension and pain are the consequences of such blockages. As with a traffic jam in a large urban center, the normal flow needs to be re-established through skillful measures. Correctly chosen, carefully prepared food can fill up your energy deficiencies and dissolve energy blockages.

IF you often feel tired, get exhausted quickly, and tend to feel cold, you will be helped by dishes that build up energy (for instance, on page 139), as well as by foods from the categories "hot" and "warm" (see the tables beginning on page 59).

IF, on the other hand, you suffer from irritation and tension or aches and pains, you will be helped by "cool" and "cold" foods, particularly those belonging to the wood element. Recipes with the note "Gives the liver new energy" (see, for instance, page 70) can help to dissolve physical and emotional tensions.

Yin and Yang in Food

The meeting of yin and yang creates new life: From the moment of conception, these forces flow through your organism. You will feel best when both energies are equally strong and balanced in your body.

IF yin predominates in your organism, you may feel
- easily cold or chilled
- tired and without energy
- as though you need warm food and warm clothing
- as though you are slightly swollen or bloated
- frequently depressed and lethargic

IF yang predominates in your organism, you may feel
- easily overheated and with a tendency toward sweating
- restless and full of nervous energy
- as though you need cool foods and lots to drink
- as though you have dry skin and nasal passages
- often tense and irritated

Too much yin leads to tiredness, lack of energy, feeling chilled, water retention, or blockages.

Too much yang leads to an excess of energy, restlessness, feelings of hotness, and dryness.

The Play of Energies

IN a healthy state, yin and yang should work together like two tennis players who want to keep the ball going as long as possible: a graceful give and take that is about harmony and not about winning. If one of the partners gains an advantage and insists on winning, the harmony is disturbed. In the human body, it can also happen that yin and yang get out of harmony. At first perhaps one or the other partner will predominate. If this condition persists, eventually yin and yang separate and give up their harmonious flow. According to its nature, yang resides in the upper body, while yin sinks toward the bottom.

After a sustained imbalance, yin and yang have separated. This leads to heat in the upper body, coldness, and lack of energy in the lower body, as well as irritation and lethargy.

When the Balance is Upset

IN the state of separated yin and yang energies you may feel
- hot and tense in your upper body
- cold and without energy in your lower body
- alternating or simultaneous cravings for warm and cold foods
- alternately or simultaneously stimulated and lethargic

THESE symptoms indicate that yin and yang already have been out of balance for some time. To bring both forces back into a harmonious flow, the best thing is to seek out a specialist in Traditional Chinese Medicine (TCM). In addition to recommendations for a balanced diet, a number of steps from the overall theory of TCM will probably be suggested to you.

TO treat already existing illnesses, specialists of TCM perform a very precise analysis to ascertain how the energies are distributed in the individual organs, or elements. Often one element will be deficient, while another will display an energy congestion. The recommended treatment is cooling for the congested element and warming for the deficient element.

A pharmacist in China prepares the medicine individually for each customer.

Traditional Chinese Medicine

FOR ages, nutritional doctors in China have been very highly respected. With the help of nutrition, excellent preventive and protective measures can be taken to enhance health.

IN the case of an acute or chronic illness, as a rule only a complex treatment plan will really be of help. Since all human beings always respond both physically as well as emotionally and mentally, the regulating measures of this type of treatment always act simultaneously on various levels: physical, mental, and emotional.

TCM's Treatment Plan

THE following methods are part of a comprehensive treatment plan according to Traditional Chinese Medicine:

- Acupuncture and moxabustion
- Herbal therapy (phytotherapy)
- Special massages (for example, *tuina*)
- Movement exercises (for example *Qi Gong*)
- Dietary recommendations

Food and the Interplay of Energies

THROUGH their reciprocal interplay, yin and yang are responsible not only for the observable phenomena of our body. All manifestations in the cosmos can be attributed to these two interdependent and interconnected forces. Our food also possesses different degrees of yin or yang. Depending on what effect a food produces in you, you can influence this yin or yang quality.

Yin Foods

FOODS containing yin are well suited to highly active, hot-blooded, forceful people. Always on the move and motivated to perform, they are constantly on a journey of discovery and often may take on more than they can handle. Relaxing and letting go, on the other hand, are difficult for them. Foods with a yin character open the door to leisure. They favor rest and refueling with new energies.

If the food contains more yin, after eating you will feel
- *calm and refreshed*
- *physically cooler*
- *hydrated*

Yang Foods

FOODS containing yang are especially good for people who often feel chilled or are easily tired or fatigued. Whether you have exhausted your energies through illness, too much work, or emotional strain, you can replenish your chi through warming foods strong in yang. Foods from the categories hot, warm, and neutral will put you back in balance. The tips for food preparation in the next chapter may also be of help.

IN climates that tend more toward coldness, there are about four times as many people with yang deficiency as with yin deficiency. Your body will let you know: When you feel pleasantly warm, the composition of your food is correctly balanced.

If the food contains more yang, after eating you will feel
- *warm and stimulated*
- *physically warmer*
- *drier in your skin and mucous membranes*

Classification of Foods

EVERY food can be naturally classified according to its yin or yang content. Dry foods that make you feel hot while eating them (for example, chile peppers) are high in yang. Moist foods that refresh and cool you (for example, melon) are high in yin. In TCM, the yin and yang properties of a food are called thermics. Starting on page 59, you will find a classification of the most important foods according to yin (cool) and yang (hot). Foods with balanced thermics (equal amounts of yin and yang) appear in the column marked "neutral."

By heating your food, you increase its yang content.

Preparation of Food

YOU can influence the yin or yang content of a food by the way you prepare it. This enables you to enjoy foods which otherwise would not be suitable for your type.

Increasing Yang

To increase the yang energy in a food with a high yin content, you should
● chop the food into small pieces before cooking (see page 57)
● introduce heat by means of boiling or frying
● reduce moisture through longer heating times
● add spices with a yang character (for example, fresh ginger)

Increasing Yin

To increase the yin energy in a food with a high yang content, you should
- keep cooking times short
- add moisture (yin), for example, in the form of tasty sauces
- add herbs with a yin character (for example, cooling fresh mint)

Food acquires more yin through the addition of liquids.

Listen to Your Body

Do you remember how people used to eat in the old days? Many of these eating habits correspond to the Chinese model of yin and yang.

Your body will show you whether you need more yin or more yang in your diet. Reward your body for its service to you by giving it more attention. Many people feel the urge to eat more fruit and salads in the summer, while in the winter they crave hot drinks, warm soups, and slowly simmered stews.

Your body has its own wisdom and clamors for a balance between yin and yang. Most of the planet's traditional cultures possess knowledge of this natural regulation. Even in Europe, many families cultivated these habits through the middle of the 20th century.

The Five Elements in the Body

Wood, fire, earth, metal, and water: From the Chinese perspective, all forms manifested in the cosmos are composed of these five elements. Thus, your body also is composed of these five energies.

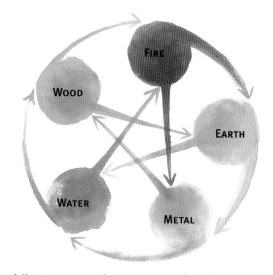

The Feeding and Restraining Cycles

WHEN you are in a healthy state, all five elements are equally represented in your body. These feed each other reciprocally with energy and ensure that no individual element becomes too pronounced.

THE outer circle of this cycle shows a clockwise energy flow. Each element feeds the element following it with energy. And each element restrains the element following the one next to it from becoming too dominant (inside arrows). Thus all five elements are interconnected in a variety of ways.

ELEMENT	ORGAN	EMOTION	SEASON	COLOR	FORM	TASTE	DIRECTION
Wood	Liver Gallbladder	Anger	Spring	Green Blue	High Cylindrical	Sour	East
Fire	Heart Small intestine	Joy	Summer	Red	Sharp Pointed	Bitter	South
Earth	Spleen Pancreas Stomach	Worry	Late Summer	Ochre Yellow	Flat	Sweet	Center
Metal	Lungs Large intestine	Grief	Autumn	White	Round	Spicy	West
Water	Kidneys Bladder	Fear	Winter	Black	Wavy	Salty	North

What Do the Elements Do in the Body?

THE table with the correspondences of the five elements shows you all the different things you can influence with certain tastes in your food: Sour tastes support your liver-gallbladder system and reduce anger and irritability. In some European countries they have the saying that "Sour makes merry." Sour herring helps a hangover by easing the liver and clearing the mind. Bitter tastes give your heart energy and make your spirit joyful. Just think, for instance, of a good cup of coffee. It stimulates the heart and circulatory system and lifts your mood. Sweet tastes feed your "center:" They calm the spleen, pancreas, stomach, and give you hopeful thoughts. Hot, spicy foods nourish the lungs and large intestine. Sad or depressed feelings start to dissipate, while endings or new beginnings become possible. Finally, salt strengthens the kidneys and gives you a sense of security and hopefulness.

All of the Elements are Important

NOW you can see why your diet should be as balanced as possible. By including each of the five tastes in your food, you supply each of the elements and thus provide for all of your major organs and emotions.

The Five Elements in Nature

FOR each season there is one element that has particular sway over the forces of the cosmos. Your body and spirit also register the element's influence. Surely you have noticed how some illnesses or moods occur with particular frequency at a certain time of year, for instance, hayfever in the spring, asthma and colds in the fall, depressions likewise in the fall, and kidney and bladder infections in the winter.

IF you observe the natural growth rhythms of plants, you will discover that they correspond to the cycle of the five elements. Many plants or fruits grow precisely in the season of their element. Nature has provided for her creatures: The food grows exactly when it is most needed.

DANDELION tonifies the liver, belongs to the wood element, and grows in the spring. Cabbage supports the kidneys, has its main season in winter, and supplies people with necessary vitamins in the cold time of year. Only people who subscribe to modern import-export strategies and consume all foods at all times of the year break this rhythm. How much better to follow nature and let oneself be supported by her endless wisdom.

The taste of a food shows you to which element it belongs. Sour foods belong to the wood element, bitter ones to fire, sweet ones to earth, spicy ones to metal, and salty ones to water.

High-Quality Food—
Careful Preparation

In traditional China, cooks were especially revered. The kitchen and eating area were the center of the community. Joint enjoyment of a good-quality, balanced meal helped peace, harmony, and health to flourish within the family.

As the Cook, So the Food

A cook—so it was believed in old China—brings his or her spirit to the food he or she prepares. The more loving, mature, and conscious the cook, the more beneficial the meal prepared with his or her hands. For this reason, in Buddhist monasteries only monks who had attained a certain level of advancement in their development were permitted to serve in the kitchen. The monastery's head chef had the task of managing food supplies "as if they were gold." He was supposed to work with awareness, care, concentration, and dignity. As a reward, his service gave him the opportunity for further growth.

THE more joy in the kitchen, the more delicious and nurturing the food .

"Love and care for others renew the heart."
(Chinese Proverb)

Cooking in the
5-Element Cycle

IN order to supply all organs and emotions with the elements they need, you should include all five elements in every dish. Be sure while you are cooking to follow the rhythms of the cycle of the elements. In TCM this very conscious art of food preparation is called "Cooking in the Cycle."

ALL the recipes in this book are composed in the cycle of the elements. By transforming the recipes into gourmet meals, over time you will become increasingly familiar with the element cycle. Incidentally, the more often you pass through this cycle in the process of cooking, the more the dynamic energy in your food increases.

Forms and Colors—
Feeding the Eye as well
as the Stomach

EACH of the five elements also has a color (see table on page 48) and a form attributed to it. These also play a role in the kitchen.

WOOD   FIRE   EARTH   METAL   WATER

For example, by using different types of knives you can cut up your vegetables and fruit according to the form attributed to the element. An attractively prepared and presented dish stimulates the digestive juices and awakens anticipation of the coming enjoyment (feeding the eye as well as the stomach). Deep inside, most people understand the symbolic meaning of form and color. Modern surveys have shown that people in Western countries intuitively understand the traditional Chinese system of correspondences of the elements.

So let your meal be a festival for the senses, and start the festival with your cooking preparations. After all, pleasurable anticipation of the meal and openness toward eating support the digestive process and leave a luminous trace of memory, so to speak, for both you and your guests!

Cooking as a Celebration

In the same way that you create an increasingly harmonious and comfortable atmosphere in your kitchen and eating area according the ideas of Feng Shui, you can also increase your own pleasure and mindfulness while cooking. Then the inner and the outer come more and more into harmonious attunement. Your life force chi flows evenly and intensifies your positive feelings.

Learning from Children

Have you ever noticed how carefully and happily children help out in the kitchen, if you let them? Children can show us the right attitude, the spirit of the Tao. Devoted, joyful, and patient, using all their senses, they practice and practice until they are successful. For them everything is a voyage of discovery, even failures and mistakes. Cooking and baking are a party. And the resulting meal is a further celebration.

Concentrated and full of joy, children are happy to help in the preparation of meals.

Nourishment as Thanks to Your Body

For most people, achieving health and well-being is an important goal.

Your Target State

You will know you've reached your target state when you
- feel happy and full of energy
- have a comfortable body temperature
- feel a harmonious balance with yourself and your environment

Getting to Know Yourself

If you have not yet or have only infrequently experienced the pleasure of this kind of living, it's worth the trouble of finding your way there. Step by step, with patience, you will be able to integrate more harmony into your life. The Chinese tradition thinks highly of serenity and much less highly of coercion and self-righteousness. "A journey of a thousand miles begins with a single step," says an old Chinese proverb. By setting out on the journey, you undertake a voyage of discovery to yourself. Who am I? What is good for me? What do I crave, even though it's not good for me? How does my body indicate its wishes to me? What keeps me from fulfilling these wishes? Can I and do I want to make changes in my life?

Concrete Objectives Make the Path Easier

"I'd like to, but…," you may be thinking as you read these lines. Does your objective have enough attractive force for you? You might take a few minutes and put together in your imagination a truly wonderful goal. It should be shining, radiant, attractive, so that you really feel like moving toward it and find solutions for every if, and, or but. Would you like a little taste?

It is (month) of (year)… (when do you want your objective to be a reality?) You see yourself in your home, which, thanks to the suggestions of Feng Shui has become happy, bright, and inviting. You enter the kitchen, joyfully anticipating the time you will spend there cooking. In your kitchen you feel completely at ease. You are happy about the foods that you will now prepare. You pick up first one food, then another, sniff it, admire form and color, and thank Mother Earth for her gifts. You think of your family, for whom you are going to cook, or of your guests, or perhaps simply of lovingly planning an evening with yourself. You feel that you're worth it, and that your guests or your loved ones at home are worth it, to be gifted with attention and love. You are glad to take time for this and have managed to arrange your daily schedule to accommodate it. Everything flows. You have banished hecticness and pressure from your life and enjoy your vitality and *joie de vivre*.

Flowers create a soft, sensual atmosphere. Their chi has a particularly nurturing quality.

In this state, of course, you have no trouble preparing a delicious meal.

FINALLY, you imagine yourself and perhaps also your guests enjoying this healthy, nourishing, flavorful food. You hear the appreciative remarks, inhale the fragrance of all the delicacies, admire the harmonious presentation, and, most of all, enjoy the happy radiance that you can feel and see in yourself and your guests. The inner and the outer are in harmony. Your body thanks you with health and energy.

TOO beautiful to be true? If you decide to take the first step today, then one day your journey of a thousand miles will bring you to your goal.

What Kind of Food is Right for You?

SELECT your foods and their mode of preparation according to the principles of energetic balance, so that your energies are always in harmony with each other.

ACCORDING to the rules of TCM, food should
- be nutritionally balanced
- create an energetic balance
- be seasonal and locally produced

Energetic Balance in Food

HOW can you tell if your food has a good energetic balance? Your body is a self-regulated, interconnected system. With admirable intelligence, it compensates for long-term consequences of poor nutrition, stress, or environmental pollution. But if you deprive it of sufficient attention and care for too long, it begins to send you tell-tale signals:
- chronic emotional disturbances
- cravings for particular foods
- illnesses
- fatigue, lethargy, and/or sleep disturbances
- feelings of stress and/or irritation
- frequent conflicts in interpersonal relationships

THESE signs have the function of a stop sign in traffic. If you stop, look around you, and then continue driving with heightened attention, you will help your organism regain its balance. A well-balanced diet gives you fitness, a pleasant body temperature, and contentedness. On the other hand, cravings and feelings of coldness shortly after eating indicate an energy deficiency.

"Your food should fit you like a well-cut suit."
(Chinese proverb)

How to Do It

YOUR food will be charged with energy if you
● buy fresh, organically grown products from farms in your area
● eat at least one cooked meal a day (in case of fatigue, weakness, lethargy, or long-term illness, make it two to three warm meals a day)
● use frozen foods only in exceptional cases, as a small portion of your total diet (cold weakens your water element, even if you thaw and reheat the food to compensate)
● abstain from using microwave ovens
● favor foods heavier in yang (see pages 59 and following), if you are a yin type
● favor foods heavier in yin (see pages 59 and following), if you are a yang type
● try to use only monounsaturated fats (for example, cold-pressed nut oils, olive oil, canola oil, and avocados)
● make sure you have enough alkaline foods in your diet (alkaline foods are, for instance, vegetables, grains, rice, potatoes, sprouts; examples of acidic foods are alcohol, meat, bread, coffee, tea, and sweets)
● enjoy variety in your diet
● take time and leisure for the preparation and enjoyment of your meals

Nutritional Values

IN the Chinese tradition, unlike in Western medicine, the composition of foods with respect to their nutritional components is not important. Vitamin, trace element, protein, or carbohydrate content are of little interest. Nutritional value only makes sense when it is utilized by the body. Which foods your organism can best utilize depends on your constitution (yin or yang).

FOR example, the carrot, of great value in nutritional terms, will pass through your body undigested if, as a yin type, you produce too little "digestive heat" in the upper belly. In order to be able to utilize any of the good nutrients at all, you need to perform a kind of "pre-digestion" by chopping up and lightly cooking the vegetable. A very simple observation shows you what you need. After you've eaten, do you feel flatulent, bloated, or lethargic? Then the food wasn't sufficiently "pre-digested," in other words, cooked.

THE supposedly usual "energy low" after a meal only indicates an energy deficit in the food. A properly composed five-element meal (charged with yang for the yin type and charged with yin for the yang type) will make you feel so energetic that you are happy to continue your work after eating. You feel well nourished and satisfied instead of lethargic and "stuffed."

Rest, a balanced, energy-filled diet, and a healthy lifestyle ensure a total sense of well-being.

Make Sure You Are Getting Enough Chi

THE life force chi is the elixir that gives you energy, joy, and happy relationships. From the traditional Chinese point of view, every human being receives a certain amount of chi at birth, as a legacy for his or her life path. When it is used up, his or her life is over. But the chi can be recharged again and again with good air and good food. However, too much work, worry, conflict, overuse of stimulants and drugs, long-term stress, insufficient sleep, environmental toxins, etc. use up the chi especially quickly.

IF you would like to lead a long and, above all, healthy life that is filled with energy, the thousand-mile journey to the Feng Shui of Five-Element Cooking will repay your efforts. Start out with small steps—each day with energy-charged food strengthens and protects you. A little is better than nothing at all.

The Five-Element Rules

FOR most people, three simple rules with regard to the five-element diet are useful:

● Strengthen your center with generous amounts of cooked food from the Earth categories Neutral, Warm, and Hot (see list on page 61)
● Protect your chi legacy by avoiding frozen foods and by eating enough foods from the Water categories Neutral, Warm, and Hot (see list on page 63)
● Refresh and tonify your liver-gallbladder system with refreshing and cooling foods from the Wood element (see list on page 59)

The Family at the Dining Table

All families are different. For example, around your dining table there may be a moody husband, insomniac wife, rebellious toddler, or lethargic teenager. Five-Element Cooking can help balance these conflicting moods.

Individuality and Community

So you've decided to take your first steps toward the balanced Five-Element diet. Congratulations on your resolution! Even if, for a while at least, you may sometimes need to call on all your creative resources—the results will repay your efforts many times over.

Tips for Getting Started

For low energy and weakness, you should protect and support your system. Helpful for this are:
- Generous amounts of cooked food
- Greens, lightly steamed for two to three minutes
- A cup of broth as a between-meal snack
- Warming herbs and spices
- Grains that are roasted before cooking
- A large number of small meals rather than two or three large ones
- Taking enough time to relax while you eat

For heat, an excess of temperament, and tension, you should aim to pacify and balance your system. Helpful for this are:
- Finely chopped raw salads and vegetables
- Large amounts of water between meals
- Cooling and refreshing herbs and spices
- The addition of sour tastes (lemon, cider vinegar) to your food

Nutrition in Crisis Situations

People who observe a separation of yin and yang after a long period of illness or heightened stress (heat in the upper body together with cold in the lower body) should follow the rules in the section "Yin and Yang in Food" (pages 41 and following). If your body responds to this with more heat in the lower body, foods with a high yang content (for instance, hot broth) should be taken often and in very small amounts.

Whether you cook for yourself, your family, or your friends, we heartily wish you much pleasure, relaxation, and enjoyment with the harmonious interplay of yin and yang in your kitchen. Make use of the opportunity to have an impact on your physical and emotional health and *joie de vivre*. May your loving attention and your caring efforts bear many fruits and flow back to you as the chi of love!

Kitchen Tips

Cooking should never be thought of as work, but as the fulfillment of our path. The Five-Element model fits any and all tastes or food preferences.

● If you can't find an important ingredient, select another one from the corresponding element (see tables on pages 59 and following). Be creative and spontaneous; this makes for variety in your everyday life.

● Buy a very good-quality, heavy-duty vegetable slicer, a big chef's knife, and a utility knife (small, short, and triangular) for chopping vegetables.

● When chopping vegetables, don't worry about getting absolutely perfect pieces right away. It doesn't matter if the vegetable strips are exactly the same size or a little thicker or thinner at first. For the sake of flavor, it is a good idea to develop a good cutting technique; besides, it's less strenuous and saves time.

● Shape the hand that holds the vegetable to be chopped—usually the left one—into a "tiger's paw" and pull in the thumb, so that middle joints of the fingers are at a 90-degree angle to the vegetable. The vegetable is held by the tips of the fingers and the thumb.

● When you first start out, chop no more than three to five slices of vegetable at a time, so that you don't have any difficulty holding the vegetable to be cut.

● Always cut at the level of the middle finger, leaving the tip of the knife on the cutting board and moving the knife up to the fingers with rocking movements; then move your hand back to expose more of the vegetable.

● When you're first starting out, don't worry about having large pieces of vegetable left over. These will come in handy for making stock.

● Whenever possible, wait until the end to add salt to anything you cook in the Water element. Salt breaks down during cooking, and flavor is lost, while the same amount of salt still needs to be processed by the kidneys. One gram of salt added at the end of cooking corresponds in flavor to 7 grams of salt that were cooked the entire time. Our kidneys and liver are the main organs responsible for detoxifying our bodies, and they deserve our special attention.

● Not all fats are the same. High-grade fatty acids are more easily metabolized than low-grade fats. Sweet, unsalted butter gives the best results in terms of flavor, but please note that butter should not be frozen.

● Truly high-quality food needs to be bought fresh. Avoid frozen and microwaved foods.

● Every stove has its own idiosyncrasies. Check the oven temperature with an oven thermometer before you start baking or roasting, to find out what setting you need to use in order to get a particular temperature. Good luck, and enjoy!

Chopping vegetables or herbs works best if you form your hand into a "tiger's paw."

INGREDIENTS

The following tables give the attribution of the most common foods to the five elements wood, fire, earth, metal, and water. The cool (yin) or warm (yang) qualities of the foods are also indicated.

If you feel weak, cold, and tired, you should consume more yang foods, and if you feel restless or overly hot, you should eat more yin foods. In this way you can ensure a balance between the polar energies yin and yang and thus support your health.

You can supply individual, perhaps weakened organs with energy by choosing neutral foods from the element to which the organ is attributed (see table on page 48).

Each season corresponds to one of the five elements. In the summer, for example, choose foods mostly from the fire element; in winter, from the water element, and so forth (see table on page 48). In this way you will ensure your organs of an optimum energy supply.

You can increase the health benefits of your meals by making sure that while you are cooking you add ingredients according to the feeding cycle (see graphic on page 48). The important thing is not to skip any element. The more often you complete the cycle—wood (Wo), fire (F), earth (E), metal (M), water (Wa)—while cooking, the more energy-charged your meal will be. The overall composition will be more harmonious and of greater energetic value.

If you wish to make ingredient substitutions in the recipes, make every attempt to select ingredients from the same element and temperature range as the one(s) you wish to replace. Use the charts on pages 59-63 as a guideline.

WOOD 火 土 金 水 *sour*

Yang ← ⟶ *Yin*

hot	warm	neutral	cool	cold
SPICES/ CONDIMENTS Vinegar (more than 7% acid content) **HERBS** Hyssop **MEAT/FISH** Crayfish Freshwater shrimp Lobster Spiny lobster **BEVERAGES** Spirits (more than 64 proof)	**SPICES/ CONDIMENTS** Balsamic vinegar Wine vinegar Yeast **HERBS** Basil Nettle **VEGETABLES** Leeks **NUTS/SEEDS** Hazelnuts Sesame seeds **FRUITS** Cherries Lychees Passionfruit Raspberries **MEAT** Pork liver **BEVERAGES** Sweet wines	**HERBS** Chervil Lemon balm Parsley Sorrel Tarragon **GRAINS** Spelt **VEGETABLES** Butternut squash Sweet potatoes **FRUITS** Grapes Plums Tangerines **MEATS** Beef liver **BEVERAGES** Chardonnay (Italian and American) Off-dry wines	**HERBS** Borage Dill **VEGETABLES** Beans Celery Lettuce Sauerkraut **FRUITS** Apples Blackberries Blueberries Gooseberries Lemons Oranges Red and black currants Sour cherries Strawberries **OILS** Sesame oil **DAIRY PRODUCTS** Sour cream **MEATS/POULTRY** Chicken Duck Veal liver **BEVERAGES** Dry wines Hibiscus tea Mallow tea Rosehip tea Sour cherry juice	**VEGETABLES** Arugula Bamboo shoots Chard Cucumbers Dandelion greens Pickles Spinach Tomatoes **FRUIT** Carambola Grapefruit Kiwi Pineapple Rhubarb **DAIRY PRODUCTS** Cottage cheese Kefir Yogurt **MEATS/POULTRY** Duck liver Goose liver Rabbit **BEVERAGES** Champagne Very dry wines

FIRE 火 土 金 水 木 *bitter*

Yang ← → *Yin*

hot

SPICES/ CONDIMENTS
Angelica root
Fenugreek
Galangal
Horseradish
Juniper berries
Nutmeg
Saffron

GRAINS
Kasha (roasted buckwheat groats)

HERBS
Lemon grass
Lemon leaves

MEATS
Grilled meats

BEVERAGES
Cognac
Hot mulled wine
Madeira
Port
Syrah

warm

SPICES/ CONDIMENTS
Bitter chocolate
Cocoa
Capers
Poppy seeds
Sweet Hungarian paprika

GRAINS
Amaranth
Buckwheat
Flaxseed

NUTS
Almonds

VEGETABLES
Brussels sprouts
Cardoons

FRUITS
Apricots
Sloe plums
Sweet cherries

MEATS/POULTRY
Chicken liver
Goat
Lamb

BEVERAGES
Black tea
Burgundy
Coffee
Grand Cru Bordeaux
Green tea

neutral

SPICES/ CONDIMENTS
Paprika

VEGETABLES
Celery root
Mâche (lamb's lettuce)
Radicchio

FRUIT
Bilberries

MEATS
Beef heart
Pork heart
Veal sweetbreads

BEVERAGES
Barbaresco
Barolo
Burgundy
Premier Cru Bordeaux
Rioja

cool

VEGETABLES
Artichokes
Beets
Belgian endive
Chicory
Iceberg lettuce
Olives
Sweet potatoes

FRUITS
Elderberry
Grapefruit
Quince

GRAINS
Oats
Red Camargue rice
Wheat

BEVERAGES
Cherry juice
Dark beer
Pilsner beer
Wheat beer

cold

VEGETABLES
Arugula
Asparagus
Cucumbers
Dandelion greens
Kohlrabi

FRUITS
Pomegranates

GRAINS
Bulgur
Couscous
Oat flakes
Wheat flakes

BEVERAGES
Beaujolais
Chianti

Yang ⟵ ☯ ⟶ *Yin*

hot	warm	neutral	cool	cold
SPICES/ SWEETENERS Anise seeds Consommé Fennel seeds Honey Licorice Malt sugar Molasses Raw (turbinado) sugar **BEVERAGES** Liqueurs Sauternes Tokay	**SPICES/ SWEETENERS** Chocolate Jam Malt Marzipan Vanilla **VEGETABLES** Fennel Green and red bell peppers Okra **FRUITS** Apricots Currants Raisins **GRAINS** Spelt Sticky rice **NUTS/SEEDS** Cashew nuts Oil-bearing seeds Pine nuts Walnuts **MEATS/DAIRY** Beef Eggs Egg yolks **BEVERAGES** Fennel tea	**JELLING AGENTS** Gelatin Pectin **HERBS** Chervil **GRAINS/GRAIN PRODUCTS** Corn Cornmeal (polenta) Millet Quinoa Spelt Tofu **VEGETABLES** Broccoli Carrots Cauliflower Chestnuts Potatoes Sweet potatoes Zucchini **FRUITS** Dates Figs Grapes Mirabelle plums **MEATS** Turkey Veal **BEVERAGES** Malt beer Sweet Boiled Water (see page 126)	**HERBS** Dill **GRAINS / GRAIN PRODUCTS** Arborio rice Barley Bread Millet Noodles and pasta Rye Sweet short-grain rice **VEGETABLES** Avocados Beans Garbanzo beans Lentils Lettuce Peas Snow peas Sweet potatoes **FRUITS** Apples Coconut Papayas Pears **OILS** Corn oil Olive oil Sesame oil Sunflower oil **DAIRY PRODUCTS** Butter Cheese Cream Milk **MEAT PRODUCTS** Lard **BEVERAGES** Fruit juice Vegetable juice	**SPICES/ SWEETENERS** Confectioners' sugar Granulated sugar **VEGETABLES** Chanterelles Iceberg lettuce Morels Napa cabbage Oyster mushrooms Porcini mushrooms Pumpkin Salsify White mushrooms **FRUITS** Bananas Mangos Watermelon

METAL 水木火土 *spicy*

Yang ⟵   ⟶ *Yin*

hot	warm	neutral	cool	cold

hot

SPICES/ CONDIMENTS
Allspice
Anise seeds
Cayenne pepper
Chile pepper
Chili powder
Cinnamon
Curry powder
Galangal
Ginger
Horseradish
Star anise
White pepper

HERBS
Hyssop
Lemon grass

MEATS
Aged venison

BEVERAGES
Spirits

warm

SPICES/ CONDIMENTS
Bay leaves
Black pepper
Cardamom
Cloves
Coriander seeds
Cumin
Ginger
Mustard

HERBS
Chives
Lovage
Thyme

NUTS
Unsalted and roasted peanuts

OILS
Canola oil

DAIRY PRODUCTS
Blue cheese
Muenster cheese

VEGETABLES
Garlic
Leeks

MEATS / POULTRY
Chicken (free-range)
Cornish hen
Partridge
Pheasant
Quail
Wild boar
Wild duck
Young venison

BEVERAGES
Sake

neutral

HERBS
Garden cress
Nasturtium
Savory

VEGETABLES
Celery root

FRUITS
Peaches

MEATS / POULTRY
Goose

cool

HERBS
Watercress

GRAINS
Long-grain rice

VEGETABLES
Daikon radish
Green onions
Kohlrabi
Onions
Pearl onions
Radishes
Shallots

cold

HERBS
Peppermint

VEGETABLES
Sweet onions
Turnips

62

WATER　木火土金　*salty*

Yang ⟵   ☯   ⟶ *Yin*

hot	warm	neutral	cool	cold
SPICES / CONDIMENTS Cinnamon Fenugreek **VEGETABLES** White truffles **MEATS/FISH** Caviar Crayfish Ham Lobster Perch Salami Salmon Shrimp Smoked fish Spiny lobster Trout Venison	**SPICES / CONDIMENTS** Caraway seeds Cloves Sea salt Star anise Table salt **SEEDS** Pumpkin seeds Sesame seeds **VEGETABLES** Black truffles Eggplant Fennel **FRUITS** Cherries Raisins Raspberries **DAIRY PRODUCTS** Blue cheese **EGGS** Egg yolks **MEATS/FISH** Cod Eel Goat Lamb Mackerel Pork Squab Sturgeon Tuna	**ADDITIVES** Agar-Agar Binding agent **GRAINS** Millet Quinoa Wild rice **VEGETABLES** Butternut squash Chestnuts Carrots **FRUITS** Grapes Plums **MEATS/FISH/ SEAFOOD** Carp Clams Grayling Herring Perch Redfish Sardines Snails Whitefish	**VEGETABLES** Dried beans Garbanzo beans Green beans Lentils Savoy cabbage Soybeans, black and yellow **OILS** Sesame oil **DAIRY PRODUCTS** Butter Cream Cream cheese Goat's milk **MEATS / POULTRY / FISH/SEAFOOD** Cod Duck Flounder Haddock Saltwater eel Sea bass Sole Squid Turbot Veal kidney **EGGS** Egg whites	**SPICES / CONDIMENTS** Miso Soy sauce Worcestershire sauce **GRAINS** Bulgur Couscous Wheat flakes **VEGETABLES** Bean sprouts Red cabbage Sea vegetables White cabbage **MEATS/FISH/ SEAFOOD** Fish stock King crab Octopus Oysters Shark Veal brains **BEVERAGES** Mineral water

WOOD ELEMENT

Spring—the dynamic energy of new beginnings! Sour-tasting foods refresh and revitalize. Tension, irritability, and anger subside, your muscles relax, and you are able to take deep breaths and find new solutions to your problems.

The recipes of this element feed your liver/gallbladder system. This, in turn, activates your metabolism and awakens your vitality. If you feel drained or fatigued, you should serve salads and fruits lightly warmed to assist the body with its digestion.

Cook foods from the wood element if you:

- have a compromised liver/gallbladder system

- often feel nervous and irritable

- frequently feel impatient or hotheaded

- have problems with your muscles, tendons, or eyes

- want to take special care of yourself in the springtime

Sorrel Soup

relaxes the liver

Yield: 4 portions

18 ounces fresh sorrel

1 bunch fresh Italian parsley

1/2 bunch fresh chervil

1 bunch fresh dill

Paprika

1 tablespoon unsalted butter

Pinch of sugar

1 heaping tablespoon flour

Freshly ground black pepper

1 quart chicken stock

Sea salt

2 tablespoons sour cream

1 tablespoon fresh lemon juice

2/3 cup heavy cream

4 hard-boiled egg yolks

Boiled potatoes (optional)

PREPARATION TIME: 1 HOUR

CAREFULLY wash and pick through the herbs, discarding any that are wilted. Put the sorrel (Wo), parsley (Wo), and chervil (Wo) in a tall, narrow container and sprinkle with a dash of paprika (F). Add the dill (E) and puree the mixed herbs using a hand blender.

PUT a saucepan over medium heat (F) and melt the butter (E). Add the sugar (E) and flour (E), and stir for several minutes. Add the pureed herbs (E) and simmer, stirring occasionally, for 5 minutes. Season to taste with pepper (M) and add the chicken stock (Wa). Sprinkle with a pinch of sea salt (Wa) and carefully beat in the sour cream (Wo) with a wire whisk.

WHISK in the lemon juice (Wo). Season with a small pinch of paprika (F) and let the soup simmer for 15 minutes.

STIR the cream (E) into the soup. Finely chop the egg yolks (E), distribute among 4 soup bowls, and then fill with the soup. Season to taste with pepper (M) and sea salt (Wa) and serve. For a complete meal, serve with the boiled potatoes.

Arugula Soup

1/2 bunch fresh chervil

8 ounces fresh arugula

1 bunch fresh Italian parsley

2 carrots

1 leek

2 1/4 pounds baking potatoes

1/2 organic lemon

4 juniper berries

4 allspice berries

1 quart chicken stock

2/3 cup dry white wine

2 tablespoons unsalted butter

Freshly ground black pepper

Freshly grated nutmeg

Sea salt

2 tablespoons crème fraîche

PREPARATION TIME: 1 HOUR

purifies and strengthens the wood element

CAREFULLY wash the chervil, arugula, and parsley. Reserve a few leaves of chervil and parsley for garnish, and finely chop the rest. Wash and peel the carrots, then slice them into thin rounds. Cut the leek in half lengthwise, wash it, and slice it into half-rings. Peel and wash the potatoes and slice them, not too thinly. Squeeze the juice from the lemon.

PUT the chopped herbs (Wo) and 2 of the juniper berries (F) in a saucepan. Add the carrots (E), potatoes (E), leek (M), and allspice (M). Pour in the chicken stock (Wa), lemon juice (Wo), and white wine (Wo). Add the remaining 2 juniper berries (F), and bring to a boil. Reduce the heat and simmer, uncovered, for 20 minutes.

REMOVE the juniper berries and mash about one third of the potatoes with a potato masher, until the soup turns creamy. Stir in the butter (E), plenty of pepper (M), nutmeg (M) to taste, sea salt (Wa) to taste, and the crème fraîche (Wo). Garnish the soup with the remaining chervil and parsley leaves (Wo).

Stuffed Tomatoes

refreshes the liver and the lungs

Yield: 4 portions

4 large, ripe tomatoes

1 pound spinach

1 bunch fresh Italian parsley

1 carrot

1 small zucchini

6 shallots

1 tablespoon unsalted butter

Freshly grated nutmeg

4 anchovy fillets, oil or brine packed

1 tablespoon wine vinegar

1/2 teaspoon paprika

4 teaspoons olive oil

Freshly ground black pepper

Sea salt

PREPARATION TIME: 30 MINUTES

PREHEAT the oven to 250°F. Wash the tomatoes, and cut the tops off. Place the tomatoes in a baking dish, and put in the oven for 2-3 minutes. With a paring knife, remove the tomato peels, and hollow out the tomatoes with a teaspoon. Set the tomato flesh aside.

WASH and drain the spinach and the parsley. Put 8 spinach leaves and 8 parsley leaves aside. Finely chop the rest of the parsley. Peel the carrot and slice it into thin rounds. Cut off the ends of the zucchini, wash it, and chop into small cubes. Peel all of the shallots and slice them into rings.

PUT a skillet over medium heat (F) and melt the butter (E). Sauté the zucchini (E), carrots (E), and shallots (M) in the butter. Add a little nutmeg (M) to the skillet. Finely chop the anchovy fillets (Wa) and add them to the vegetable mixture.

ADD the spinach (Wo), parsley (Wo), vinegar (Wo), and the tomato flesh (Wo) to the skillet and sauté until the moisture has evaporated. Spoon this filling into the hollowed-out tomatoes. Garnish with parsley (Wo) and spinach leaves (Wo) and sprinkle with the paprika (F). Drizzle with the olive oil (E) and season the stuffed tomatoes to taste with pepper (M) and salt (Wa).

Refreshing Green Salad

gives the liver new energy

Yield: 4 portions

2 heads butter lettuce

1 bunch fresh Italian parsley

2 tablespoons water

1/4 cup balsamic vinegar

1/2 teaspoon paprika

1/2 cup olive oil

Small piece of red chile (depending on degree of spiciness desired)

1 tablespoon mustard

Sea salt

PREPARATION TIME: 25 MINUTES

REMOVE the tough outer leaves and core from the lettuce heads, wash them, and spin them dry. Tear the lettuce leaves into bite-sized pieces. Wash, dry, and finely chop the parsley.

IN a large salad bowl, mix the water (Wa) with the balsamic vinegar (Wo), paprika (F), and olive oil (E). Finely chop the chile (M) and add it to the bowl.

ADD the mustard (M) and season the dressing with sea salt (Wa). Put the chopped parsley (Wo) and the lettuce (Wo) into the bowl, toss everything well, and serve.

Roasted Bulgur with Parsley

a source of strength and energy

Yield: 4 portions

8 ounces bulgur wheat

4 carrots

1 onion

1 bunch fresh Italian parsley

1 teaspoon paprika

2 teaspoons green peppercorns

Freshly ground black pepper

Sea salt

2 1/2 cups water

1 organic lemon

1 sprig fresh rosemary

1 tablespoon olive oil

PREPARATION TIME: 1 HOUR

PICK through the bulgur and discard any little stones or husks. Wash and peel the carrots, and cut them into fine strips (or shred them). Peel the onion and cut it into cubes. Wash, dry, and finely chop the parsley.

PUT the bulgur (Wo) in a saucepan with a dash of paprika (F) and put over medium heat (F). Roast the bulgur for 10-15 minutes, stirring constantly. The grains may show light-brown speckles.

ADD the finely sliced carrots (E), the onion cubes (M), and the green peppercorns (M). Season to taste with black pepper (M) and sea salt (Wa), and add the water (Wa). Wash and dry the lemon. Grate the zest, or strip it off with a zester, and squeeze the juice. Add the lemon zest (Wo) and juice (Wo) to the wheat mixture to taste. Put the rosemary (F) on top of the wheat and cook, covered, for 15-20 minutes. Remove from the heat and let the mixture stand for 10 minutes. Serve the wheat on plates and drizzle with the olive oil (E).

Shrimp Skewers

Yield: 4 portions

16 large fresh shrimp

8 brown mushrooms

8 medium-sized cherry tomatoes

8 miniature corncobs

10 cloves garlic

8 ounces Basmati rice

8 green olives, pitted

Dash of paprika

2 tablespoons unsalted butter

1 carrot

Freshly ground black pepper

Sea salt

2 cups water

1 organic lemon

1 teaspoon saffron threads

In addition:

8 wooden skewers, soaked in oil

PREPARATION TIME: 1 HOUR 10 MINUTES

new energy for liver and kidneys

PREHEAT the oven to 150°F. Remove the bristle at the tail end of each shrimp, if present. Make a light incision down the back of each shrimp and remove the dark intestine. Wipe the mushrooms clean and cut off the stems. Wash the tomatoes and remove the stems. Pat dry the miniature corncobs. Peel the garlic.

PICK through the rice and remove any grains that are blemished. On each oiled wooden skewer, thread 1 mushroom (E), 1 corncob (E), 1 garlic clove (M), 2 shrimp (Wa), 1 cherry tomato (Wo), and 1 olive (F). Set the skewers in two skillets and place over medium heat. Sprinkle the skewers with the paprika (F) and add the butter (E). Chop the rest of the garlic (M) and sprinkle over the skewers. Sauté the skewers for 5 minutes on each side, until the shrimp is cooked through, and keep them warm in the oven.

WASH, peel, and cut the carrot into julienne strips. Put a pot on the fire and sprinkle in some paprika (F). Add the carrot strips (E) and the rice (M). Pan-roast the rice and carrot for 10 minutes, stirring constantly. Season with pepper (M) and salt (Wa), then add the water (Wa). Grate the lemon zest, then squeeze the juice. Add the zest and juice (Wo) to the pot according to taste. Sprinkle in the saffron (F) and cook for 10 minutes with a slightly opened lid. Turn off the heat and let the rice stand for 10 minutes. Serve the skewers over the rice.

Celery and Tomato Ragout

dissolves stagnation in the wood element

Yield: 4 portions

1 organic lemon

1 2/3 cups water

4 juniper berries

1 bunch celery

2 carrots

2 baking potatoes

1 bunch fresh basil

1 bunch fresh chives

1 onion

8 tomatoes

2 tablespoons unsalted butter

Freshly ground black pepper

8 ounces mozzarella cheese

Dash of paprika

PREPARATION TIME: 50 MINUTES

WASH the lemon, grate the zest, and squeeze the juice. Add the water (Wa) to a saucepan and put on the stove with a little of the lemon zest (Wo) and 1 of the juniper berries (F). Wash the celery, separate the stalks, and cut off the ends. Wash the carrots, peel them, and cut into julienne strips (or shred them). Put the vegetable peels in the pan. Wash, peel, and dice the potatoes. Wash, dry, and finely chop the basil and the chives. Peel the onion and add the peel to the pot (M). Dice the onion. Add a little more water (Wa) to the pot if necessary to cover the vegetable peelings, and bring to a simmer. Simmer the stock for a few minutes; drain before using.

WASH the tomatoes (Wo), cut into slices, and arrange in a baking dish. Slice the celery stalks (Wo) and put them in a saucepan. Sprinkle with the basil (F) and the rest of the juniper berries (F). Put the butter (E) in the middle of the pan, then add the potatoes (E), carrots (E), onion (M), and chives (M) in layers. Season to taste with pepper (M), pour in the stock (Wa), and cook for 12-15 minutes. Remove the vegetables with tongs and arrange them over the tomatoes in the baking dish. Cook down the stock a little and pour it over the vegetables in the dish.

PREHEAT the oven to 225°F. Cut the mozzarella (Wo) into slices and arrange over the vegetables. Sprinkle with the lemon juice, grated lemon zest (Wo), and paprika (F). Bake for a few minutes, until the vegetables are heated through and the cheese is melted.

Green Beans with Cherry Tomatoes

builds up body fluids

Yield: 4 portions

14 ounces cherry tomatoes

20 ounces fresh green beans

1 bunch fresh Italian parsley

1 zucchini

4 shallots

4 cloves garlic

2 tablespoons unsalted butter

1/2 cup water

1 organic lemon

Dash of paprika

Dash of freshly grated nutmeg

1 tablespoon hot mustard

Sea salt

1 tablespoon crème fraîche

8 coriander seeds

Freshly ground white pepper

2 tablespoons olive oil

PREPARATION TIME: 1 HOUR

WASH the cherry tomatoes, beans, parsley, and zucchini. Cut each tomato in half and remove the stem. Trim the tips and ends of the beans and slice them on the diagonal. Slice the zucchini once lengthwise, and then cut crosswise into strips. Peel and mince the shallots and the garlic. Chop the parsley.

PLACE a saucepan on the stove over medium heat (F). Put the butter (E) in the pot and let it melt. Add the minced garlic and shallots (M) and sauté until they turn golden brown. Add the water (Wa).

SQUEEZE the lemon and add the juice (Wo) to the pan, reserving 1 tablespoon. Add a dash of paprika (F) and add the cut-up beans (E). Season the beans with the nutmeg (M) and the mustard (M), stir, cover, and cook for 3-4 minutes. Stir again and let simmer, covered, for another 4 minutes.

SPRINKLE with a little sea salt (Wa), then add the halved tomatoes (Wo), crème fraîche (Wo), parsley (Wo), and coriander seeds (F). Cook, covered, for 3 minutes. Add the zucchini strips (E) to the pot, season generously with white pepper (M), and cook for 5 more minutes. Season to taste with sea salt (Wa), the rest of the lemon juice (Wo), a dash of paprika (F), and the olive oil (E).

Tomatoes in Walnut Vinaigrette

a cooling dish for hot days

Yield: 4 portions

1/4 cup fresh lemon juice

1/2 tablespoon raw (turbinado) sugar

Freshly ground black pepper

Sea salt

8 large tomatoes

2 bunches fresh basil

2 carrots

2 onions

2 tablespoons water

1/2 teaspoon paprika

6 tablespoons extra-virgin olive oil

1/4 cup chopped walnuts

PREPARATION TIME: 25 MINUTES

FILL a pot with water (Wa), add some of the lemon juice (Wo), and bring to a boil (F). Add the raw sugar (E), ground pepper (M), and salt (Wa) to taste.

WASH the tomatoes, score them cross-wise, dip them briefly in the boiling water, and slip off the skins. Slice the tomatoes (Wo) and arrange them on serving plates.

WASH the basil and the carrots. Pluck the basil leaves (F) off of the stems and arrange them over the tomato slices. Trim the carrots, peel them, and cut or shred them into fine strips. Peel and dice the onions. Distribute the carrots (E) and the onions (M) evenly over the tomato slices.

DRESS each serving with 1/2 tablespoon of the water (Wa), 1 tablespoon of the lemon juice (Wo), a little paprika (F), 1 1/2 tablespoons of the olive oil (E), and 1 tablespoon of the chopped walnuts (E). Just before serving, season to taste with pepper (M) and salt (Wa).

Chicken Livers with Braised Greens

Yield: 4 portions

4 bunches arugula

1 head radicchio

20 green olives, pitted

4 cloves garlic

8 shallots

1 bunch green onions

2 sprigs fresh thyme

1 cup short-grain rice

1 2/3 cups water

2 tablespoons balsamic vinegar

1 tablespoon unsalted butter

2 teaspoons sesame seeds

12 chicken livers

1 tablespoon small capers

Dash of paprika

Freshly ground black pepper

1 tablespoon grainy mustard

1 tablespoon sour cream

2/3 cup red wine

PREPARATION TIME: 45 MINUTES

tonifies blood and body fluids

THOROUGHLY wash and trim the arugula, reserve 16 leaves for garnish, and finely chop the rest. Quarter the radicchio, then wash and spin-dry. Quarter the olives.

PEEL the garlic and shallots, cut them in half, and slice thinly. Wash the green onions and the thyme. Trim the onions and cut them on the diagonal into 1 1/4-inch pieces. Heat a saucepan over medium heat (F), pick through the rice (E) to remove any small stones or other debris, then pan-roast it for about 10 minutes, stirring frequently. Chop the thyme (M) and add it to the pan. Pour in the water (W) and 1 tablespoon of the vinegar (Wo), and cook the rice, covered, for about 18 minutes.

PREHEAT the oven to 150°F. Heat a skillet over medium heat (F), melt the butter (E), and brown the shallots (M) and garlic (M) in the butter. Sprinkle with some of the sesame seeds and sauté the chicken livers (Wo) for about 4 minutes on each side. Remove the livers from the skillet and keep them warm in the oven.

ADD the radicchio (F) to the skillet and braise for 2 minutes on each side. Add the olives (F), capers (F), paprika (F), and chopped arugula (F). Season to taste with pepper (M), and add the mustard (M) and onions (M). Stir in the remaining sesame seeds (Wa), sour cream (Wo), vinegar (Wo), and red wine (F). Serve the braised greens with the sautéed chicken livers and rice. Garnish with the reserved arugula leaves.

Duck Breasts in Red Currant Sauce

Yield: 4 portions

8 ounces fresh red currants

4 ounces fresh chervil or Italian parsley

2 carrots

4 large boiling potatoes

2 cloves garlic

1 shallot

1 onion

1 bay leaf

1 2/3 cups water

Small piece of zest from an organic lemon

4 small or 2 large duck breasts

2 tablespoons unsalted butter

Sea salt

1 teaspoon wine vinegar

Dash of paprika

4 juniper berries

2 tablespoons heavy cream

2 tablespoons mustard

Freshly ground black pepper

PREPARATION TIME: 1 1/2 HOURS

cools and moistens the wood element

PREHEAT the oven to 150°F. Wash the red currants, chervil, carrots, and potatoes. Peel the potatoes and the carrots. Dice the potatoes (E), and put them in a saucepan. Slice the carrots (E) and put them on top of the potatoes. Peel the garlic, shallot, and onion. Dice the onion (M) and add it to the pot. Add the bay leaf (M), water (Wa), and lemon zest (Wo) and bring the liquid to a boil (F). Reduce the heat and simmer for about 15 minutes, until the potatoes are tender. Put the pan in the oven to keep warm.

SCORE the duck breasts on the fatty side in a crisscross pattern. Strip the currants off the stems and chop the chervil. Put a skillet over medium heat (F). Melt the butter (E) in the skillet, then halve the garlic (M) and the shallot (M) and add them to the skillet. Sprinkle with a little sea salt (Wa). Place the duck breasts (Wo) skin-side down in the skillet and sauté for 15-20 minutes, until the skin turns crisp. Turn them over and add the chervil (Wo) to the fat in the pan. Cook the meat for 8 more minutes. Transfer the duck to a plate and put it in the oven to keep warm.

PUT the red currants (Wo), vinegar (Wo), paprika (F), and juniper berries (F) in the pan, stir in the cream (E) and mustard (M), and heat through. Season generously with pepper (M) and remove from the heat. Add salt (Wa) to taste and distribute the sauce among four plates. Arrange the duck breasts over the sauce and top with the stewed potatoes and carrots.

Fresh Raspberries with Crème Fraîche

Yield: 4 portions

strengthens the liver and kidneys

1 pound raspberries

1 pound strawberries

2 tablespoons confectioners' sugar

Dash of ground allspice

Sea salt

1/2 cup crème fraîche

Cocoa powder

PREPARATION TIME: 40 MINUTES

SORT through and clean the raspberries and strawberries. Remove the stems from the strawberries (E) and put them in a tall mixing bowl with the confectioners' sugar. Sprinkle with the ground allspice (M) and a little sea salt (Wa). Puree the mixture with a hand blender, and distribute the sauce among 4 serving plates.

PUT 2 tablespoons of the crème fraîche (Wo) in the middle of each plate, use a toothpick to smooth it into a heart shape, and arrange the raspberries (Wo) on top. Sprinkle with a trace of cocoa powder (F).

VARIATION:

You can prepare other fruits in this manner, such as orange "fillets." To fillet the oranges, cut off the top and bottom the oranges, and, with a sharp knife peel them in such a way that the white pith stays on the peel (not on the fruit). Put a sieve over a bowl and, holding the fruit over the sieve, cut out the individual fillets very close to the membranes. Catch the fillets in the sieve and remove the seeds. Drink the collected juice or reserve it for another use.

Vegetable Terrine with Smoked Salmon

eases stress

Yield: 4 portions

2 grapefruits

1 red bell pepper

1 large carrot

Small piece of zest from an organic lemon

1 bunch fresh dill

2 bunches fresh chives

1 bunch fresh Italian parsley

2 sprigs fresh thyme

4 3/4 cups plain yogurt (do not use nonfat)

4 peppercorns

3 packages unflavored gelatin

Freshly ground white pepper

Sea salt

10 slices smoked salmon

Mint leaves to garnish

PREPARATION TIME: 1 1/2 HOURS, PLUS 4-6 HOURS FOR THE GELATIN TO SET

PEEL and fillet the grapefruits, reserving the juice (see page 80 for instructions on filleting citrus fruits). Wash and cut the red pepper in half, then seed and dice it. Wash, peel, and dice the carrot. Mince the lemon zest. Wash and spin-dry the dill, chives, parsley, and thyme. Finely chop the washed herbs.

PLACE 6 tablespoons of the yogurt (Wo) in a small saucepan with 2 of the peppercorns (M) and sprinkle with 1 1/2 packages of the gelatin (E). Let stand for about 5 minutes. Heat the mixture gently (F), stirring, until the gelatin is dissolved. Off the heat, stir in half each of the red pepper cubes (E), carrot cubes (E), dill (E), chives (M), and thyme (M). Season to taste with pepper (M), sea salt (W), and half of the minced lemon zest (Wo); stir in 2 cups of the yogurt (E).

ARRANGE the smoked salmon (Wa) in the bottom of a terrine mold. Cover with the yogurt-gelatin mixture, spreading evenly, and half of the grapefruit fillets (Wo). Chill in the refrigerator for 2-3 hours, until set. Prepare the remaining ingredients in the same manner as the first vegetable-yogurt mixture, pour over the solidified layer, and chill for 2-3 more hours, until set. Cut the terrine into slices and garnish with the mint leaves (Wo).

Sour Cherry Compote with Cream

refreshes the liver on hot days

Yield: 4 portions

20 ounces fresh sour cherries (from a jar,
if fresh are unavailable)
1 bunch fresh lemon balm or mint
Dash of paprika
1-2 tablespoons sugar
1/2 cinnamon stick
1/4 cup water
Zest of 1 organic lemon, cut into large strips
4 fresh sage leaves
2/3 cup chilled heavy cream

Preparation time: 40 minutes

Wash and pit the sour cherries (Wo), then put them in a pot. Wash the lemon balm (Wo), shake dry, and reserve a few leaves for garnish. Chop the rest of the leaves and put them in the pot with the cherries. Add the paprika (F) and put the pot over medium-low heat (F).

Stir in the sugar (E), cinnamon stick (M), water, and lemon zest (Wo). Simmer the compote, covered, for 8 minutes. Remove the cinnamon stick and lemon zest, pour the compote into dessert dishes, and let cool. Garnish with the reserved lemon balm leaves (Wo) and sage leaves (F). Pass the cream (E) at the table.

Hot Spiced Grapes

relieves the liver

Yield: 4 portions

1 pound small white Muscat grapes
1/2 organic lemon
1/2 teaspoon cocoa powder
1 1/4 cups white grape juice
1 tablespoon heavy cream
2 pods star anise
2 tablespoons water

Preparation time: 35 minutes

Wash the grapes and remove them from the stems. Cut each grape in half and remove all of the seeds. Grate the lemon zest and squeeze the juice. Put the lemon zest and juice (Wo) as well as the grapes (Wo) in a saucepan and place over medium heat (F).

Stir the cocoa powder (F), grape juice (E), and cream (F) into the pan. Add the star anise (M) and the water (Wa). Simmer gently for 5 minutes, remove the star anise, and serve hot in dessert dishes.

FIRE ELEMENT

Summer heat—growth and ripeness! A little bit of bitter taste supports your energy in the fire element. Your heart and circulatory system find the right rhythm, and your personality unfolds joyfully. Heart and arteries are in a harmonious tension and give you the gift of happy vitality as blood is pumped through your body. With the recipes of this section you feed your heart and soul.

Cook something from the fire element if you:

- have a compromised heart or circulatory system
- would like more joy and harmony in your life
- want to refresh and build up your blood and body fluids
- would like to stimulate and vitalize your mind and spirit
- would like to take special care of yourself in the summertime

Pan-Roasted Whole-Grain Muesli

gets your day off to a cheery start

Yield: 4 portions

2 cups whole-grain wheat flakes

1 cup whole-grain oat flakes

8 dried apricots, chopped

1/4 cup raisins

Dash of ground cinnamon

Sea salt

Grated lemon zest

Cocoa powder

Splash of heavy cream (for cold variation)

PREPARATION TIME: 20 MINUTES

HEAT a skillet over medium heat and add the whole-grain wheat and oat flakes (F). Pan-roast the flakes for 8 minutes, stirring them occasionally.

COLD variation: Put the flakes (F) and apricots (F) in a bowl, then add the raisins (E), cinnamon (M) to taste, and a little sea salt (Wa), grated lemon zest (Wo), cocoa powder (F), and the cream (E).

WARM variation: Mix the flakes (F) in the pan with the apricots (F), raisins (E), cinnamon (M), sea salt (W), and a little water. Add lemon zest (Wo) and cocoa (F) to taste, and cook for 10 minutes.

Kasha Soup with Rosemary

gives your heart new energy

Yield: 4 portions

2 carrots

1 onion

4 sprigs fresh rosemary

1 1/3 cups buckwheat flour

Freshly ground black pepper

1 quart chicken stock

Fresh lemon juice

PREPARATION TIME: 25 MINUTES

PEEL and grate the carrots. Peel and mince the onion. Wash and shake dry the rosemary. Put a saucepan over medium heat (F) and toast the flour (F) for 6-7 minutes, stirring occasionally. Add the grated carrots (E), minced onions (M), pepper (M), and chicken stock (Wa). Simmer for 10 minutes with a little lemon juice (Wo) and the rosemary sprigs (F). Remove the rosemary and serve in soup dishes.

Mâche Salad with Pomegranate Seeds

Yield: 4 portions

Generous 1 pound mâche (lamb's lettuce)

2 bunches arugula

4 shallots

4 cloves garlic

6 ounces fresh green beans

2 carrots

1 pomegranate

1 tablespoon unsalted butter

2 tablespoons mild mustard

Freshly ground black pepper

Sea salt

2 tablespoons water

2 tablespoons balsamic vinegar

Dash of paprika

2 tablespoons heavy cream

2 tablespoons olive oil

Baguette (optional)

PREPARATION TIME: 45 MINUTES

THOROUGHLY wash the mâche and arugula several times and drain well. Chop the arugula. Peel and mince the shallots and garlic. Trim the beans and slice on the diagonal. Trim, peel, and cut the carrots into strips (or shred them). Cut open the pomegranate and remove the seeds (they tend to squirt, so it's best to wear an apron to protect clothing).

HEAT a skillet over medium heat (F) and add the butter (E). Add the beans (E), carrots (E), shallots (M), and garlic (M). Cover the pan and braise the vegetables for 6-8 minutes, stirring frequently. Add the mustard (M), pepper (M) to taste, salt (Wa) to taste, water (Wa), and vinegar (Wo). Dust the vegetables with paprika (F).

ADD the arugula (F) to the pan, cover, and steam for 1 minute; remove from the heat, and let cool. Put the cooled vegetables in a bowl with the pomegranate seeds (F) and the mâche (F). Add the cream (E) and the olive oil (E), and mix well. Serve the salad with the baguette, if desired.

Artichokes with Noodles

Yield: 4 portions

12 baby artichokes

Small piece of organic lemon zest

2 zucchini

1 bunch fresh Italian parsley

12 fresh sage leaves

4 cloves garlic

4 shallots

8 ounces tagliatelle (thin noodles)

2 tablespoons unsalted butter

A few green peppercorns

2/3 cup dry white wine

2 tablespoons olive oil

Freshly ground black pepper

Sea salt

PREPARATION TIME: 50 MINUTES

gives your heart strength

WASH the artichokes and remove the stems and tough outer leaves. Fill a pot with 2 quarts water (Wa), add the lemon zest (Wo), and bring to a boil (F). Reduce the heat and simmer the artichokes, covered, for 12 minutes. Remove and drain the artichokes (reserving the cooking water) and, when cool enough to handle, cut them lengthwise into thin slices.

PREHEAT the oven to 150°F. Wash and trim the zucchini and cut into julienne strips (or shred them). Wash, dry, and finely chop the parsley and sage. Peel and mince the garlic and shallots. Bring the artichoke water to a boil, add the noodles, and cook until slightly firm to the bite (*al dente*). Drain the noodles, reserving a little of the cooking water, and keep them warm in the pre-heated oven.

PUT a skillet over medium heat (F). Lay the artichoke slices (F) in the skillet, add the butter, and brown the artichokes on both sides. Add the zucchini (E), shallots (M), green peppercorns (M), and garlic (M) and briefly sauté. Pour a little of the artichoke cooking water (Wa) and the white wine (Wo) into the pan. Add the parsley (Wo), sage leaves (F), and olive oil, remove from the stove, and toss in the noodles (E). Season to taste with pepper (M) and salt (Wa).

Escarole Salad with Carrots

Yield: 4 portions

1 large head escarole

4 small onions

10 ounces carrots

1 bunch fresh chives

2 tablespoons unsalted butter

Freshly ground black pepper

2 ounces Roquefort cheese

1/4 cup white wine vinegar

2 tablespoons olive oil

4 ripe pears

2 ripe avocados

Sea salt

1 bunch fresh basil

2 tablespoons sour cream

PREPARATION TIME: 35 MINUTES

builds up blood and body fluids

REMOVE the escarole leaves from the stem, wash, shake dry, and cut into strips. Peel, halve, and mince the onions. Peel the carrots and slice them finely. Wash, shake dry, and chop the bunch of chives.

PUT a skillet over medium heat (F), melt the butter, and sauté the carrots (E) and onions for 6-8 minutes. Season with pepper (M). Add the crumbled Roquefort cheese (M/Wa) and pour in the white wine vinegar (Wo).

ADD the escarole to the skillet and toss briefly, then remove it from the heat. Drizzle the escarole mixture with olive oil (E). Peel and chop the pears (E) and avocados (E) and scatter them over the salad along with the chives (M). Season to taste with pepper (M) and salt (Wa). Wash the basil, shake dry, and pluck the leaves off the stems. Garnish the salad with the sour cream (Wo) and the basil leaves (F) before serving.

90

Dandelion Salad with Croutons

provides energy for the heart and liver

Yield: 4 portions

1 3/4 pounds baby dandelion greens

4 slices white bread

1 tablespoon fresh lemon juice

1 juniper berry

4 eggs

1/4 cup unsalted butter

Freshly ground black pepper

Sea salt

2 tablespoons water

2 tablespoons balsamic vinegar

Dash of paprika

2 tablespoons olive oil

1 tablespoon mustard

PREPARATION TIME: 45 MINUTES

WASH the dandelion greens very thoroughly, spin dry, then trim and chop. Cut the crusts off the bread slices, cut into cubes, and let dry in a 200°F oven.

HALF-FILL a pot with water (Wa), add a splash of the lemon juice (Wo), and bring to a boil (F). Toss in the juniper berry (F), reduce the heat, and simmer for a few moments. One at a time, carefully break the eggs into a cup, then slide them into the simmering water. Cook the eggs for 1 1/2 to 3 minutes, depending on how hard you like the yolks. With a slotted spoon, gently remove the eggs from the water and place them on a plate and keep warm.

HEAT a skillet over medium heat, melt the butter (E), and sauté the bread cubes (E) until crisp and brown on all sides. Season to taste with pepper (M) and sea salt (Wa). Remove from the skillet, and keep warm.

POUR the 2 tablespoons water (Wa) and the vinegar (Wo) to the skillet. Add the dandelion greens and braise lightly. Remove from the heat and sprinkle with paprika (F). Add the olive oil (E), mustard (M), and pepper (M) and sea salt (Wa) to taste, and mix well. Sprinkle with the rest of the lemon juice (Wo) and a little more paprika, and serve with the poached eggs and the croutons.

Breaded Celery Root

Yield: 4 portions

2 organic lemons

1 celery root

8 ounces unsalted butter

3 eggs

1 cup flour

Freshly ground black pepper

Sea salt

1 bunch fresh basil

1 clove garlic

1 shallot

2 tablespoons small capers or caperberries

Dash of paprika

1/2 cup extra-virgin olive oil

1 tablespoon hot mustard

1/4 cup water

1/4 cup balsamic vinegar

2 tablespoons heavy cream

PREPARATION TIME: 50 MINUTES

food for your fire element

WASH the lemons, grate the zest, and squeeze the juice. Put the lemon zest and juice in a large bowl. Peel and quarter the celery root, then cut the pieces into thin slices and put them in the bowl with the lemon juice. Mix well.

PUT a skillet over medium-low heat (F). Add the unsalted butter (E) and let it melt. Skim off all the white foam as it rises to the top.

BEAT the eggs (E) in a dish with a fork. Put the flour (E) in another dish. Drain the celery root slices (M), then dip first in the beaten egg, then in the flour, and fry until crisp and golden in the hot butter. Season to taste with pepper (M) and sea salt (Wa). Sprinkle with lemon juice (Wo) and keep warm in a 150°F oven.

WASH and finely chop the basil. Peel and mince the garlic and shallot. Mix the capers (F), a dash of paprika (F), the olive oil (E), minced garlic and shallots (M), pepper (M) to taste, sea salt (Wa) to taste, the mustard (M), water (W), vinegar (H), and a little more paprika (F). Stir in the basil and the cream. Serve the sauce with the fried celery root slices.

Braised Asparagus

Yield: 4 portions

24 thick asparagus spears

3 tablespoons fresh lemon juice

2 carrots

2 bunches fresh chives

1 bunch fresh Italian parsley

8 ounces cherry tomatoes

2 tablespoons unsalted butter

2 tablespoons heavy cream

Freshly ground white pepper

Sea salt

1 tablespoon paprika

2 tablespoons extra-virgin olive oil

PREPARATION TIME: 1 HOUR

food for happy hearts

WASH the asparagus and carefully peel the lower third of the stalks. Trim off the woody end on the diagonal, then cut the spears diagonally into three pieces. Half-fill a pot with water (Wa). Add a splash of lemon juice (Wo) and bring to a boil. Add the asparagus peels (F) to the pot and cook down to make an asparagus stock.

WASH the carrots, chives, parsley, and tomatoes. Peel the carrots, adding the peels to the stock, and cut the carrots into fine strips. Finely chop the chives and parsley. Remove the stems from the tomatoes, and cut them in half. Put a skillet (with a lid) over medium heat. Put the lower segments of the asparagus spears (F) in the pan, and the tips (F) on top. Put the butter (E) in the middle of the skillet, cover, and braise the asparagus for 3-4 minutes without stirring. Turn the asparagus and braise for 4 more minutes. Sprinkle in the carrot strips (E), add the cream, and cover the skillet. Reduce the heat and cook the vegetables until tender, about 5 more minutes.

ADD the chives (M), pepper (M) to taste, a little asparagus stock (Wa), sea salt (Wa) to taste, parsley (Wo), tomatoes (Wo), the remaining lemon juice (Wo), the paprika (F), and olive oil (E) and mix well.

Sweet Potato Puree

Yield: 4 portions

18 ounces sweet potatoes

18 ounces baking potatoes

2 carrots

1 onion

1 bay leaf

1 pod star anise

1/2 organic lemon

4 juniper berries

2 tablespoons unsalted butter

Freshly ground white pepper

Sea salt

2 tablespoons sour cream

A dash of paprika

Chopped fresh parsley

PREPARATION TIME: 1 HOUR

releases blockages in the fire element

WASH, peel, and slice the sweet potatoes (F), and put into a pot. Do the same with the baking potatoes (E). Peel the carrots (E), slice finely, and place on top of the sweet and baking potatoes. Peel the onion (M), slice, and put on top of the other vegetables. Add the bay leaf (M) and the star anise (M). Cover the vegetables with water (Wa).

WASH the lemon, grate the zest, and squeeze out the juice. Add the lemon zest (Wo), lemon juice (Wo), and juniper berries (F) to the pot, and bring to a boil (F). Simmer the vegetables, covered, for 20 minutes.

STRAIN the cooking liquid into another pot, and cook it down to about 1 1/4 cups. Add the butter (E) to the vegetables, season to taste with pepper (M) and salt (Wa), and pour in the reduced cooking liquid. Puree the vegetables with a potato masher. Stir in the sour cream (Wo) and the paprika (F). Garnish servings with chopped fresh parsley.

Duck Liver with Rhubarb and Fresh Figs

Yield: 4 portions

regenerates blood and body fluids

4 stalks fresh rhubarb

2 shallots

2 cloves garlic

4 ounces arugula

4 fresh figs

2 tablespoons unsalted butter

Freshly ground black pepper

Sea salt

4 duck livers

1 tablespoon balsamic vinegar

2 juniper berries

6 tablespoons water

PREPARATION TIME: 30 MINUTES

PEEL the rhubarb stalks from the bottom ends and cut them diagonally into 2-inch pieces. Peel and finely dice the shallots and garlic. Thoroughly wash and trim the arugula. Trim and quarter the figs.

PUT a skillet over medium heat (F) and melt 1 tablespoon butter (E). Put the garlic (M) and shallots (M) in a ring around the outer edge of the skillet, add a grind of fresh pepper (M) and a pinch of salt (Wa), and place the duck livers (Wo) in the middle of the pan. Sauté the livers for 4 minutes on each side, remove from the skillet, and keep warm in a 150°F oven.

ADD the rhubarb (Wo) to the skillet. Add a splash of the vinegar (Wo) and the juniper berries (F). Add the remaining 1 tablespoon butter (E) and the figs, and season to taste with pepper (M). Stir in the water (Wa), cook the mixture down a little bit, and season to taste with salt (Wa). Stir in the rest of the vinegar (Wo) to taste and distribute the mixture among 4 plates. Serve the duck livers over the rhubarb and garnish with the arugula.

Roasted Oats with Basil

Yield: 4 portions

8 ounces oat groats

2 bunches arugula

2 bunches fresh basil

10 tablespoons olive oil

4 cloves garlic

Freshly ground black pepper

Sea salt

1 onion

1 turnip

2 carrots

1 red bell pepper

1 apple (such as Gravenstein)

2 cups water

Juice of 1 organic lemon

Dash of paprika

PREPARATION TIME: 1 HOUR, PLUS 3-4 DAYS FOR SPROUTING

makes you happy and content

SOAK the oats in water overnight. The next day, pour off the water and cover the container. Rinse with fresh water every 8 hours. After 3-4 days, the grain will sprout.

WASH the arugula (F) and the basil (F). Set aside 4 sprigs each of the arugula and basil for garnish, finely chop the rest, and put in a tall container. Add 9 tablespoons of the olive oil (E), the peeled garlic cloves (M), and pepper (M) and sea salt (Wa) to taste, and puree with a hand blender.

PEEL and dice the onion and turnip. Peel the carrots and cut them into julienne strips (or shred them). With a sharp vegetable peeler, carefully peel the red pepper. Cut the pepper into 6 pieces, trim it well, and cut the pieces into small dice.

PEEL and core the apple and cut it into thin slices. Put a pot over medium heat, add the sprouted oats (F), and pan-roast for 6-8 minutes. Add the pepper cubes (E), apple slices (E), and carrots (E), as well as the diced onion and turnip (M). Pour in the water (Wa), lemon juice (Wo), and paprika (F), and cook, covered, until the vegetables are tender, about 15 minutes. Drizzle with the remaining 1 tablespoon olive oil (E), and pepper (M) and salt (Wa) to taste. Serve with the herb sauce, seasoning with a few drops of lemon juice to taste. Garnish with the reserved herb sprigs.

Stuffed Beets

revitalizes body fluids and blood

Yield: 4 portions

1 small daikon radish

2 large carrots

8 small beets

2 zucchini

2 bunches fresh Italian parsley

1 onion

1/2 cup red Camargue rice (or wheat berries)

1/4 cup heavy cream

Freshly ground black pepper

1 1/2 cups water

2/3 cup white wine

Dash of paprika

Sea salt

1 tablespoon fresh lemon juice

PREPARATION TIME: 1 1/2 HOURS

PEEL the daikon radish, carrots, and beets. Cut the "lids" off the beets. Cut the daikon radish and carrots into small dice. Hollow out the beets with a melon baller, leaving the sides and bottoms whole. Cut the removed beet flesh into small dice. Wash and dice the zucchini. Wash and dry the parsley. Arrange a few of the parsley leaves in circles in 4 deep dishes, and chop the rest. Peel and dice the onion.

PICK over the rice to remove any blemished grains, put it in a pot over medium heat (F), and toast it for 7-8 minutes. Add 1 tablespoon of the cream (E) and pepper to taste (M), and pour in 1 cup of the water (Wa). Cook the rice, covered, for about 15-20 minutes, until all of the liquid is absorbed. Turn off the heat and let the rice stand, covered, for 10 more minutes.

MIX the remaining 1/2 cup water (Wa) and the white wine (Wo) and divide between 2 saucepans. Sprinkle both with a dash of paprika (F). Put the pots over medium-high heat (F). Put the hollowed-out beets (F) in one pot and steam for 5 minutes; then add the cubed beets (F) and steam for 3 more minutes. Remove the beets from the pot, keep warm, and cook down the cooking liquid to a sauce consistency. Stir and add in the remaining 3 tablespoons cream (E). Meanwhile, cook the diced carrots (E), zucchini (E), daikon radish (M), and onions in the other pot, for 5 minutes. Remove the vegetables from the pot and cook down the cooking liquid to a sauce consistency.

SEASON the beets and the sauce with pepper (M). Add the diced beets to the other vegetables, season the mixture with salt (Wa), and sprinkle with a little lemon juice (Wo). Stir in the parsley. Stuff the hollowed-out beets with the vegetable mixture and serve them over the rice, garnished with the two sauces.

Marinated Lamb Chops

energy for heart and liver

Yield: 4 portions

12 lamb chops

1 bunch fresh rosemary

1 bunch fresh thyme

8 cloves garlic

8 olives

4 juniper berries

1/2 cup olive oil

1 tablespoon black peppercorns

1 pod star anise

2 tablespoons water

Grated zest of 1 organic lemon

Dash of paprika

Freshly ground black pepper

Sea salt

Cooked potatoes as accompaniment (optional)

PREPARATION TIME: 45 MINUTES, PLUS 24 HOURS FOR MARINATING

REMOVE most of the fatty layer on each lamb chop (F) and put the chops in a glass baking dish. Wash the rosemary and thyme, and peel the garlic cloves. Pit and chop the olives. Put the rosemary (F), juniper berries (F), olive oil (E), peppercorns (M), star anise (M), garlic (M), thyme (M), water (Wa), lemon zest (Wo), chopped olives (F), and a dash of paprika in the baking dish with the lamb chops, and toss to coat the chops with the marinade. Cover and refrigerate for 24 hours, turning the chops frequently.

PREHEAT the oven to 150°F. Place a skillet over medium heat (F). Remove the lamb chops (F) from the marinade and put in the skillet. Sauté the chops until golden brown, about 5-6 minutes on each side. Keep warm in the oven. Add a little of the marinade to the pan and simmer, stirring, to make a sauce. Serve the lamb chops with the sauce. Season with pepper (M) and salt (Wa) to taste. Serve with potatoes, if desired.

Gratin of Cardoons

lifts your spirits

Yield: 4 portions

4 tomatoes • 2 stalks celery

2 large cardoons • 4 large potatoes

2 carrots • 2 onions

Curry powder • Sea salt

2 cups chicken stock • 2 tablespoons crème fraîche

Dash of paprika • 2/3 cup heavy cream

**PREPARATION TIME: 45 MINUTES, PLUS
1 1/2 HOURS FOR BAKING**

WASH and slice the tomatoes and celery. Peel the cardoons, potatoes, and carrots, then cut them into slices. Peel and slice the onions. Preheat the oven to 325°F .

IN a baking dish, layer the tomatoes (Wo), cardoons (F), potatoes (E), celery (E), carrots (E), and onions. Sprinkle each layer with a small amount of curry powder (M) and salt (Wa) to taste. Pour over the stock (Wa) and crème fraîche (Wo), and sprinkle the top with paprika (F). Pour the cream over the top and bake the gratin for 1 1/2 hours. Let it stand for a few minutes before serving.

Brussels Sprouts with Almonds

energy for your heart

Yield: 4 portions

28 ounces Brussels sprouts

1 onion

8 ounces sliced almonds

2 tablespoons unsalted butter

1/4 cup heavy cream

8 coriander seeds • Sea salt

Fresh lemon juice • Dash of paprika

PREPARATION TIME: 35 MINUTES

WASH, halve, and trim the Brussels sprouts. Peel and dice the onion. Put the Brussels sprouts (F), sliced almonds (F), and butter (E) in a saucepan and braise until the sprouts are tender, but still slightly firm, about 8-10 minutes.

ADD the cream (E), coriander seeds (M), and diced onions (M) to the Brussels sprouts and mix well. Remove the pot from the heat. Season the sprouts to taste with sea salt (Wa), lemon juice (Wo), and a little paprika (F).

Chicken Heart Skewers

Yield: 4 portions

24 chicken hearts

8 whole fresh chestnuts

8 pearl onions

8 cherry tomatoes

5 stalks lemon grass

1 organic lemon

1 tablespoon fenugreek seeds

1/2 cup short-grain rice

1 tablespoon dry mustard

1 cup water

1 walnut-sized piece fresh ginger

Curry powder

Sea salt

Dash of paprika

2 tablespoons unsalted butter

PREPARATION TIME: 45 MINUTES

pleasing to the eye; good for the heart

RINSE and drain the chicken hearts. Preheat the oven to 400°F. Score the chestnuts crosswise, arrange on a baking sheet, and roast in the oven for 15 minutes; remove them from the oven and pull off the peels using a paring knife. Peel the onions. Wash the tomatoes and remove the stems.

WASH and halve the lemon grass stalks lengthwise. Diagonally cut off the ends from 8 of the halved stalks, and chop one stalk finely. Wash the lemon, grate the zest, and squeeze the juice. Place a saucepan over medium heat and add the chopped lemon grass (F). Add the fenugreek seeds (F) and rice (E) and toast for 10 minutes, stirring occasionally.

SPRINKLE the rice with the dry mustard (M) and pour in the water (Wa). Add a small amount each of the grated lemon zest (Wo) and lemon juice (Wo), and cook the rice, covered, until done, about 15-20 minutes. Keep warm in the oven.

CUT the ginger into 8 slices. Thread 3 chicken hearts (F) on each of the lemon grass skewers, then 1 chestnut (E), 1 slice of ginger (M), and 1 onion (M). Sprinkle with the curry powder (M), sea salt (Wa), and paprika, and finish with 1 tomato (Wo) each. Put the skewers in a skillet, add the rest of the lemon juice (Wo) and zest (Wo) according to taste, and put on the stove (F) over medium heat. Add the butter (E) to the skillet and sauté the skewers on both sides until done. Serve over the rice.

EARTH ELEMENT

Harvest time—a sweet pleasure. Sweet tastes tranquilize, create a good mood, pacify, and enhance a harmonious community.

A well-nourished stomach makes us feel good and distributes the energy evenly to all the cells of our body. And the connective tissue provides unity. The recipes for this element help to balance your body, mind, and soul.

Cook yourself something from the earth element if you:

- often feel tired and drained of energy
- have an unsettled feeling in the stomach, and show signs of turbulence or pressure
- have problems with your connective tissue
- often brood and worry
- want to take special care of yourself in late summer

Barley Soup with Vegetables

Yield: 4 portions

4 carrots

1 small leek

1/4 celery root

2 onions

8 ounces pearl barley

1 organic lemon

2 juniper berries

1 1/2 quarts chicken or vegetable stock

Dash of paprika

4 egg yolks

2/3 cup heavy cream

Freshly ground white pepper

Dash of freshly grated nutmeg

Sea salt

PREPARATION TIME: 40 MINUTES

supports your earth element

WASH, peel, and dice the carrots. Cut the leek in half lengthwise, wash well, and cut into slices. Peel, wash, and dice the celery root. Peel and dice the onions.

RINSE the barley (Wa) well and put into a saucepan. Wash the lemon and grate a little bit of the zest. Squeeze the juice. Add the lemon zest (Wo) and the juniper berries (F) to the barley, and pan-roast for 12 minutes over medium heat. Add the celery root (F), carrots (E), leek (M), and onions (M), and sauté briefly. Pour in the stock.

ADD the lemon juice (Wo) and paprika (F) to the soup. Cover the pot and simmer for 15 minutes. Stir the egg yolks (E) and cream (E) together until blended. Remove the soup from the stove, let cool a little, and then stir in the egg-cream mixture. Sprinkle with pepper (M) and nutmeg (M) and season to taste with sea salt (Wa).

Salsify Salad with Brown Mushrooms

strengthens the spleen and pancreas

Yield: 4 portions

2 bunches fresh chervil

2 bunches fresh chives

2 onions • 1 clove garlic

10 ounces brown mushrooms

18 ounces small potatoes

28 ounces salsify

3 tablespoons white wine vinegar

2 tablespoons paprika

Freshly grated nutmeg

1 bay leaf

1 tablespoon allspice berries

1 cup water

2 cups chicken stock

2 tablespoons unsalted butter

Freshly ground white pepper

Sea salt • 3 egg yolks

1 tablespoon hot mustard

PREPARATION TIME: 2 1/2 HOURS

WASH the chervil and the chives. Peel the onions and the garlic. Chop the herbs, garlic, and 1 of the onions. Wipe clean the mushrooms. Wash and peel the potatoes.

CLEAN the salsify with a brush, peel the stalks (wear gloves, as they stain), and slice on the diagonal. Put 2 tablespoons of the vinegar (Wo) and 1 tablespoon of the paprika (F) in a bowl and mix with the salsify (E).

PUT the remaining onion (M) in a saucepan with a sprinkling of grated nutmeg (M), the bay leaf (M), allspice (M), water (Wa), stock, and the remaining 1 tablespoon vinegar (Wo). Add the remaining 1 tablespoon paprika (F) and the salsify (E) mixture, bring to a boil, and simmer for 5 minutes.

PUT a skillet over medium-high heat (F), add the butter (E), and heat until foamy. Add the mushrooms (E), sprinkle with the chopped onion (E) and garlic (M), and sauté the mushrooms until softened, about 12 minutes. Add the potatoes (E) to the pot with the salsify and simmer until tender, about 25 more minutes. Strain the cooking liquid into another saucepan and cook it down until it measures about 1 1/4 cups. Distribute the mushroom mixture among 4 plates and season to taste with pepper (M) and salt (Wa).

ADD the egg yolks (E), chives (M), pepper (M) and salt (Wa) to taste, mustard (M), and reduced stock (Wa) to the salsify and potatoes, mix well, and sprinkle with the chopped chervil (Wo). Serve the salsify mixture with the mushrooms.

Snow Pea Salad

Yield: 6 portions

18 ounces snow peas

2 carrots

2 zucchini

2 onions

4 tart apples

3 tablespoons fresh lemon juice

Paprika

4 ripe pears

Freshly ground black pepper

1 tablespoon unsalted butter

Dash of curry powder

Sea salt

1 tablespoon pumpkin seed oil

2 tablespoons balsamic vinegar

1 tablespoon heavy cream

PREPARATION TIME: 35 MINUTES

feeds your earth element

WASH the snow peas and trim off the ends. Peel the carrots and wash the zucchini. Cut both into fine julienne strips. Peel and finely dice the onions.

PEEL, halve, and core the apples (Wo), slice them finely, and put in a bowl. Pour the lemon juice (Wo) over the apples and mix well. Sprinkle with a dash of paprika (F). Peel, halve, and core the pears, slice them finely, add them to the bowl with the apples, and season to taste with the ground pepper (M).

PUT a skillet over medium heat (F) and melt the butter (E). Add the snow peas (E), zucchini, carrot strips (E), and diced onions (M). Season the vegetables to taste with pepper (M), stir well, and sauté for 5-7 minutes, until the vegetables are tender-crisp. Transfer the vegetables to a bowl and cool.

STIR in the sliced apples and pears. Add the curry powder (M), sea salt (Wa) to taste, pumpkin seed oil (Wa), vinegar (Wo), a dash of paprika (F), and the cream (E) and mix well.

Sautéed Oyster Mushrooms

tonifies the blood

Yield: 4 portions

2 bunches fresh Italian parsley

1 bunch fresh chives

2 sprigs fresh rosemary

4 shallots

6 cloves garlic

20 ounces oyster mushrooms

1 1/4 cups short-grain rice

2 1/3 cups water

2 tablespoons unsalted butter

Freshly ground black pepper

Sea salt

2 tablespoons balsamic vinegar

PREPARATION TIME: 40 MINUTES

WASH and shake dry the parsley, chives and rosemary. Reserve a few parsley sprigs for garnish. Chop the rest of the parsley and the chives. Peel and mince the shallots and garlic. Wipe clean the mushrooms and slice them.

SORT through the rice. Put a saucepan over medium heat (F), add 1 sprig of the rosemary (F) and the rice (E). Toast the rice for 8 minutes, stirring occasionally. Add 1/4 of the minced shallots (M), 1 2/3 cups of the water (Wa), and 1/4 cup of the chopped parsley (Wo), and simmer, covered, for about 15 minutes, until all of the cooking liquid is absorbed. Turn off the heat and let the rice stand for 5 minutes.

MEANWHILE, put a skillet over medium heat (F) and add the butter (E). Add the mushrooms (E), the remaining 3/4 of the shallots (M), and the garlic (M), and sauté for 12 minutes. When everything is nice and brown, season to taste with pepper (M) and salt (Wa), and stir in the remaining 2/3 cup water (Wa). Add the balsamic vinegar (Wo) and the remaining sprig of rosemary. Simmer the mixture briefly so that it thickens slightly, remove the rosemary. Stir in the chives, and serve the mushrooms and sauce with the rice. Garnish with the reserved parsley sprigs.

Baked Stuffed Potatoes with Avocados

Yield: 4 portions

4 baking potatoes

3 carrots

2 stalks celery

1 bunch fresh Italian parsley

2 tablespoons fresh marjoram

1 1/4 cups water

2 tablespoons mustard

Freshly ground white pepper

8 ounces Muenster cheese, shredded

Small piece of organic lemon zest, grated

Dash of paprika

1/4 cup heavy cream

1/4 cup unsalted butter

2 ripe avocados

Sea salt

PREPARATION TIME: 1 HOUR, 30 MINUTES

nourishes your earth element

PREHEAT the oven to 400°F. Scrub the potatoes well, pierce them several times with a fork, and place them in the oven directly on the oven rack. Bake them for about 1 hour, until they are tender.

MEANWHILE, wash the carrots, celery, parsley, and marjoram; shake the herbs dry. Reserve a few sprigs of parsley for garnish; chop the rest of the parsley and the marjoram. Peel the carrots; chop the carrots and celery. Remove the potatoes from the oven and let stand until cool enough to handle. Cut off the tops of the potatoes with a knife. With a spoon, carefully remove the potato flesh, leaving a sturdy, 1/4-inch shell. Place the removed potato flesh in a bowl.

REDUCE the oven heat to 300°F. Place the carrots (E), celery (E), and water in a saucepan and simmer until tender, about 5-10 minutes. Strain and add the vegetables to the bowl with the potato flesh. Add the mustard (M), pepper (M), cheese (M/Wa), lemon zest (Wo), paprika (F), chopped parsley (Wo), and marjoram (F), and mix well. Add the cream (E) and mix well. Fill the potato shells with the potato-vegetable mixture (you may have extra) and place the filled potatoes on a baking sheet. Top the filled potatoes with pats of the butter (E) and bake for about 15 minutes, until heated through.

JUST before serving, peel the avocados (E), slice them, and arrange over the potatoes. Season to taste with pepper (M) and salt (W), and garnish with the reserved parsley sprigs.

Zucchini Chips with Olive-Oil Mayonnaise

Yield: 4 portions

8 medium zucchini

2 sprigs fresh thyme

1 organic lemon

4 cloves garlic

Freshly ground black pepper

4 tablespoons sesame seeds

4 sprigs fresh rosemary

2 tablespoons unsalted butter

4 egg yolks

3/4 cup extra-virgin olive oil

1 tablespoon hot mustard

Sea salt

1/4 cup sour cream

Dash of paprika

PREPARATION TIME: 25 MINUTES, PLUS 1 HOUR BAKING TIME

a celebration for every cell of the body

WASH, trim, and finely slice the zucchini (E) lengthwise (use a vegetable slicer or mandoline for best results), and divide between two parchment-covered baking sheets. Wash the thyme (M), pluck the leaves off the stems, and sprinkle the leaves over the zucchini. Wash the lemon, grate the zest, and squeeze the juice. Preheat the oven to 275°F.

PEEL and mince the garlic (M) and sprinkle 3/4 of it over the zucchini. Season to taste with pepper (M), then sprinkle with the sesame seeds (Wa), grated lemon zest (Wo), and the rosemary (F). Top with pats of the butter (E) and bake the zucchini in the oven until crisp, about 1 hour.

IN a bowl, beat the egg yolks (E) well with a whisk or hand blender. While beating, slowly add the oil (E), at first drop by drop, then in a slow drizzle. Stir in the mustard (M), then season to taste with pepper (M) and salt (Wa). Add lemon juice (Wo) to taste, stir in the sour cream (Wo), and sprinkle with paprika (F). Serve with the zucchini chips.

NOTE: If you are concerned about the raw eggs in your area, you can substitute 1/2 cup pasteurized frozen egg yolks for the fresh egg yolks. Leftover mayonnaise stays fresh, covered, in the refrigerator for several days.

Potato-Mushroom Gratin

Yield: 4 portions

18 ounces mushrooms

2 1/4 pounds baking potatoes

2 bunches green onions

Dash of paprika • 2 egg yolks

1 cup heavy cream

Freshly ground black pepper

8 ounces Gorgonzola cheese

3 tablespoons crème fraîche

1 tablespoon olive oil • Sea salt

PREPARATION TIME: 50 MINUTES, PLUS 1 1/4 HOURS BAKING TIME

provides moisture and energy

WIPE clean the mushrooms and slice them. Peel the potatoes and cut them into fine slices. Trim, wash, and cut the green onions into rings. Preheat the oven to 300°F.

SPRINKLE the paprika (F) into a baking dish and arrange the potatoes (E) and mushrooms (E) in layers in the dish. In a bowl, beat the egg yolks (E) with the cream (E) and pour over the vegetables. Top with the onions (M), pepper (M) to taste, crumbled Gorgonzola (M/Wa), and crème fraîche (Wo), spreading evenly. Bake the gratin for 1 1/4 hours (F). Drizzle with the olive oil (E), and season to taste with pepper (M) and salt (Wa) before serving.

Quinoa with Champagne

Yield: 4 portions

1 small head green cabbage • 2 shallots

8 ounces quinoa • 2 allspice berries

1 1/4 cups water

1 cup Champagne (or water)

Small piece of organic lemon zest

2 juniper berries

2 tablespoons extra-virgin olive oil

Pinch of curry powder • Sea salt

PREPARATION TIME: 40 MINUTES

power for your earth element

QUARTER the cabbage and remove the core. Wash the cabbage and shred it. Peel and dice the shallots. Put a pot on the stove (F), add the quinoa (E), and toast for 5 minutes, stirring the grain frequently.

ADD the shallots (M), allspice (M), cabbage (Wa), water (Wa), and Champagne (Wo) to the pot and stir well. Add the lemon zest (Wo) and juniper berries (F) and simmer for 10-15 minutes, until all the liquid is absorbed. Stir in the olive oil (E), curry powder (M), and salt to taste (Wa) and mix well before serving.

Vegetable "Risotto" with Arugula and Dill

gives your earth element a boost

Yield: 4 portions

2 bunches arugula

2 bunches fresh dill

1 leek

2 onions

1 clove garlic

1 carrot

1 zucchini

1 1/4 cups short-grain rice

1 tablespoon mustard seeds

Freshly ground white pepper

1 2/3 cups water

1 tablespoon white wine vinegar

1 tablespoon unsalted butter

Sea salt

PREPARATION TIME: 40 MINUTES

WASH, trim, and chop the arugula, dill, and leek. Peel and mince the onions and garlic. Wash the carrot and the zucchini. Peel the carrot, and shred or finely slice the carrot and the zucchini.

PICK through the rice (E) to remove any blemished grains, and toast it in a saucepan over medium heat for 10 minutes, stirring occasionally. Add the carrot (E), zucchini (E), onions (M), garlic (M), leek (M), mustard seeds (M), pepper (M), water (Wa), and white wine vinegar (Wo), cover the pan, and cook the rice for 12 minutes.

TURN off the stove and stir in the arugula (F), dill (E), and butter (E). Let stand, covered, for 5 minutes. Season the mixture to taste with pepper (M) and sea salt (Wa).

Vegetable Sushi

builds up body fluids

Yield: 4 portions

2 large carrots

1 English (seedless) cucumber

1 bunch green onions

1 1/4 cups sushi rice or short-grain rice

Freshly ground white pepper

1 2/3 cups water

Sea salt

1 tablespoon rice vinegar (or

mild white wine vinegar)

1 package nori (pressed seaweed sheets)

10 thin slices prosciutto (optional)

Wasabi paste

Dash of paprika

Soy sauce

PREPARATION TIME: 1 1/4 HOURS

PEEL the carrots and the cucumber. Cut the carrots and the cucumber into long strips. Trim and wash the green onions.

PICK through the rice (E) to remove any blemished grains, and toast it in a saucepan over medium heat for 8 minutes, stirring constantly so that the rice doesn't change color. Season with pepper (M) and pour in the water (Wa). Cover the pot and cook the rice for 12-15 minutes, without lifting the lid. Turn off the stove and let the rice stand, covered, for 5 minutes. Let the rice cool, then season to taste with salt (Wa), and stir in the rice vinegar (Wo).

SPREAD out the nori sheets (Wa) on a large cutting board with a kitchen towel or bamboo mats underneath, and place 1 slice of prosciutto (Wa) (if using) in the middle of each nori sheet. Leave a 1-inch border on each end. Distribute the rice (Wo) over the prosciutto and pat it smooth.

ARRANGE the cucumber (Wo), carrots (E), and green onions in a strip down the center of the rice (M). Spread with a small amount of wasabi (M), and sprinkle with paprika (F), and a touch of sea salt (Wa). With the help of the kitchen towel or bamboo mat, roll up the nori sheet around the filling and press it firmly into a roll. Slice the rolls crosswise with a very sharp knife, dipping it in cold water between cuts. Serve with dishes of additional wasabi (M) and

Potato Puree with Truffle Oil

builds up yin

Yield: 4 portions

4 juniper berries

3 1/3 pounds baking potatoes

2 onions

1 clove garlic

1 bay leaf

2 cups water

Small piece of organic lemon zest

Paprika

1/4 cup unsalted butter

1 1/4 cups milk

Dash of freshly grated nutmeg

Freshly ground black pepper

Sea salt

1/4 cup sour cream

1/4 cup truffle oil (or olive oil)

PREPARATION TIME: 1 HOUR

PUT the juniper berries (F) in a pot. Wash, peel, and slice the potatoes (E), then add them to the pot. Peel and dice the onions and the garlic. Add the onions (M), garlic (M), and bay leaf (M) to the pot. Add the water (Wa) and lemon zest (Wo), and bring to a boil.

SIMMER the potatoes until tender, about 20 minutes. Strain the cooking liquid into another pan, and cook it down to about 1 cup in volume. Place the potatoes in a bowl, remove the juniper berries, and sprinkle with a dash of paprika (F). Add the butter (E) and milk (E) to the potatoes.

ADD the nutmeg (M), pepper (M), sea salt (Wa), and reduced cooking liquid (Wa), and carefully puree everything with a hand blender (take care not to overprocess the mixture). Distribute the puree among 4 plates, make an indentation in the middle of each mound, and fill each with 1 tablespoon of the sour cream (Wo). Sprinkle with a pinch of paprika (F), and drizzle 1 tablespoon of the truffle oil (E) over each portion.

Spaghetti with Snow Peas

Yield: 4 portions

1 small leek

8 ounces snow peas

2 carrots

2 small zucchini

1 onion

1 clove garlic

3 tablespoons fresh lemon juice

Paprika

16 ounces spaghetti

2 pods star anise

2 tablespoons unsalted butter

1 bunch fresh Italian parsley

Sea salt

2 tablespoons heavy cream

Freshly ground black pepper

PREPARATION TIME: 1 1/2 HOURS

a yin booster for big and small

CUT the leek in half lengthwise, wash thoroughly, and slice crosswise. Trim the tips of the snow peas, wash, and cut into strips. Peel the carrots, wash the zucchini, and cut both lengthwise into fine julienne strips.

PEEL the onion and garlic. Cut the onion in half lengthwise and slice into strips. Fill a pot with 2 quarts water (Wa), add 2 tablespoons of the lemon juice (Wo) and a dash of paprika (F), and bring to a boil (F).

ADD the spaghetti (E), garlic (M), and 1 pod of the star anise (M) to the water, and stir to keep the noodles from clumping together. Cook the spaghetti until slightly firm to the bite (*al dente*) according to the directions printed on the package.

WHILE the noodles are cooking, put a skillet over medium heat and melt the butter (E). Add the snow peas (E), carrots (E), zucchini (E), leek (M), onion (M), and the remaining pod of star anise (M), and sauté for 8 minutes. Wash and chop the parsley.

REMOVE the skillet from the heat, and season with salt (Wa). Stir in the remaining 1 tablespoon lemon juice (H), the parsley (Wo), a dash of paprika (F), the cream (E), and pepper (M) to taste. Pour the spaghetti through a colander, remove the garlic and star anise, and shake the spaghetti well to remove the liquid. Add the spaghetti to the skillet and mix with well the vegetable mixture.

Hot Mirabelle Plums with Nougat Parfait

pacifies the earth element

Yield: 4 portions

2 cups milk

1 vanilla bean • 6 eggs

5 tablespoons raw (turbinado) sugar

1 1/3 cups heavy cream

6 ounces mixed candied fruits

6 ounces nougat • Confectioners' sugar

Walnut-sized piece of fresh ginger

Pinch of sea salt

18 ounces mirabelle plums (or grapes)

2/3 cup white grape juice

Pinch of ground cinnamon

2 tablespoons water

Small piece of organic lemon zest, grated

**PREPARATION TIME: 1 1/4 HOURS,
PLUS 3 HOURS FREEZING TIME**

PLACE the milk (E) in a heavy-bottomed saucepan over medium-low heat (F). Slit open the vanilla bean (E) lengthwise and add it to the milk. In another saucepan, bring a few inches of water to a boil, then turn the heat down so that the water barely simmers. Insert a smaller pot or stainless steel bowl that fits on top of this water bath to create a double boiler (or use a double boiler if you have one). Prepare another water bath in a large bowl, using ice water.

SEPARATE the eggs (E). Put the yolks into the small pot or stainless steel bowl and beat with the sugar (E) until foamy. Remove the vanilla bean from the milk. Very slowly whisk the warm vanilla milk (E) into the egg yolk mixture. Beat constantly for about 15 minutes over the hot water bath, until the custard mixture thickens. Take care not to overheat the custard, or the egg will curdle. Then, put the pot into the ice-water bath and beat the custard for about 20 minutes, until cool.

IN a clean oil-free bowl, beat the egg whites (E) until they are very stiff. Gently fold 1/3 of the egg-whites into the cooled custard to lighten the mixture. Then, fold in the remaining egg whites, taking care not to overmix. In another bowl, whip the cream (E) until stiff and carefully fold it into the lightened custard. Chop the candied fruits (E) and the nougat (E) into small pieces, and dust with a little confectioners' sugar (E). Finely chop the ginger. Gently stir the candied fruits, nougat, ginger, and salt (Wa) into the custard mixture. Pour the mixture into a triangular or round mold (line it with plastic wrap for best results), cover, and freeze until set, about 3 hours.

WASH and pit the plums (E) (or seed the grapes if necessary), then put them in a saucepan with the grape juice (E). Add the cinnamon (M), water (Wa), and the lemon zest (Wo), and simmer for 4 minutes. Unmold the nougat parfait, remove the plastic wrap, and cut into serving slices. Serve the nougat parfait with the hot spiced fruit.

Figs in Coffee Sabayon

Yield: 4 portions

12 fresh figs

1 cup water

Small piece of organic lemon zest

2 ounces top-quality coffee beans

8 egg yolks

3 tablespoons raw (turbinado) sugar

2 tablespoons vodka,

or pinch of ground cinnamon

Sea salt

Squeeze of fresh lemon juice

Seeds from 1 cardamom pod

PREPARATION TIME: 35 MINUTES

strengthens the stomach and the heart

WASH the figs, score the tops crosswise, and pull down the peel part-way, leaving the lower part of the peels on the fruits to resemble flower blossoms.

IN a saucepan, bring the water (Wa), lemon zest (Wo), and coffee beans (F) to a boil and simmer briefly. Strain, then cook down the liquid to about 6 tablespoons.

TRANSFER the liquid to a stainless steel bowl (F) and place over a pot of simmering water (take care that the bottom of the bowl does not touch the water). Add the egg yolks (E), 2 tablespoons of the sugar (E), the vodka or cinnamon (M), salt (Wa), lemon juice (Wo), and the cardamom (F) to the bowl, and whisk constantly until the mixture is thickened and frothy. Sprinkle servings with the rest of the sugar (E), and garnish with the figs.

Stuffed Dates

new energy for the spleen

Yield: 4 portions

16 fresh dates

8 ounces marzipan

2 ounces bittersweet chocolate

8 ounces hazelnut nougat

1 cup heavy cream

Pinch of ground cinnamon

Sea salt

1 tablespoon fresh lemon juice

Cocoa powder for garnish

PREPARATION TIME: 25 MINUTES

CUT the top off of each date (E). Cut the marzipan into 8 pieces. Remove the pits from the dates and stuff each fruit with a piece of the marzipan (E). Press the tops back on the dates. **IN** a saucepan, bring a small amount of water to a simmer. Put the chocolate (F) in a stainless steel bowl and set over the pot of water. Stir until melted. Remove the bowl from the heat, add the hazelnut nougat (E), and beat the mixture with a wire whisk until blended.

POUR the cream (E) into the chocolate mixture, add the cinnamon (M), sea salt (Wa), and lemon juice (Wo), and beat with a whisk until it forms a sauce consistency. Serve the sauce with the stuffed dates (E) and garnish with the cocoa (F).

Mango Cream

aids digestion and refreshes

Yield: 4 portions

2 ripe mangos

2 1/2 cups ice-cold heavy cream • Sea salt

1/2 cup crème fraîche

1 tablespoon fresh lemon juice

2 pinches of cocoa powder

2 pinches of ground cinnamon

PREPARATION TIME: 30 MINUTES, PLUS 1 HOUR COOLING TIME

PEEL the mangos and slice the flesh off of the pits. Chop the mango flesh, puree, and refrigerate. In a bowl, whip the cream until stiff. **IN** another bowl, mix the sea salt (Wa), crème fraîche (Wo), lemon juice (Wo), cocoa (F), and the fruit puree (E). Gently fold 1/3 of the whipped cream (E) into the mixture to lighten it, then fold in the rest. Spoon the mango cream into bowls, dust with cinnamon (M), and chill for 1 hour before serving.

METAL ELEMENT

FALL —a time of change. By letting go, by giving yourself over to transformation, new energy emerges from the depths. Body, mind, and soul prepare themselves for the energizing rest of winter. Piquant spices enliven your respiratory passages. For example, an onion helps for colds, and lungs and the large intestine can regenerate themselves. If your immune system is suppressed, you will benefit from Sweet Boiled Water (page 126). When drinking this, skin cells and mucous membranes are moistened, and each cell can pass its toxins on to this water for elimination.

Enjoy foods from the metal element if you:

- have a weakened respiratory or digestive system

- have a lowered immune system

- often have problems with your skin and/or mucous membranes

- often feel sad or depressed

- want to take special care of yourself in the fall

Sweet Boiled Water

Yield: about 12 quarts

12 quarts water

4 stalks fresh Italian parsley

2 juniper berries

1 teaspoon fennel seeds

1 pod star anise

PREPARATION TIME: 40 MINUTES

detoxifies and humidifies

POUR the water (Wa) into a large saucepan with a lid. Add the washed parsley stalks (Wo), juniper berries (F), fennel seeds (E), and star anise (M), and bring it to a boil. Reduce the heat, cover the pot, and simmer for 15 minutes. **TURN** off the stove and wait 10 minutes, until the lime and the minerals bound to the water have settled. Carefully pour off the water. Drink 2-3 quarts daily. If you feel chilly, drink it hot; otherwise drink it lukewarm.

Fresh Mint Sauce

Yield: about 18 ounces

1 bunch fresh Italian parsley • 1 bunch fresh basil

2 bunches fresh mint (preferably peppermint)

1/2 cup chicken stock • 2-3 tablespoons fresh lemon juice

Dash of paprika

1 2/3 cups olive oil • 1 tablespoon mustard

Freshly ground black pepper

2 cloves garlic • Sea salt

PREPARATION TIME: 30 MINUTES

refreshing sauce for vegetables and meat

WASH, spin-dry, and pull the leaves off the parsley, basil, and mint.
TO a blender, add the stock (Wa), lemon juice (Wo), parsley (Wo), basil (F), mint (M), paprika (M), olive oil (E), mustard (M), pepper (M) to taste, and peeled garlic (M). Blend everything thoroughly, then season to taste with salt (Wa). The sauce will keep in the refrigerator for several days.

Fresh Mint Salad with Semolina

Yield: 4 portions

2 bunches fresh mint (preferably peppermint)

2 bunches fresh Italian parsley

4 tomatoes

2 shallots

1 piece red or green chile (depending on desired spiciness)

1 organic lemon

8 ounces semolina

1 tablespoon fennel seeds

Freshly ground black pepper

1 2/3 cups water

2 tablespoons buttermilk

Dash of paprika

1/4 cup extra-virgin olive oil

Sea salt

PREPARATION TIME: 45 MINUTES

builds up yin on warm days

WASH the mint and parsley, pull off a few of the nicest leaves from each, and chop the rest. Plunge the tomatoes into boiling water for a few seconds. With a paring knife, slip off the tomato skins. Remove the stems, and squeeze out the tomato seeds. Chop the tomato flesh. Peel and slice the shallots. Wash, trim, seed, and finely chop the chile. Wash the lemon and grate the zest, or strip it off with a zester. Squeeze the lemon juice.

PUT a saucepan on the stove over medium heat. Add the semolina (F) and fennel seeds (E), and toast them, stirring, for 6 minutes. Add the shallots (M), chile (M), mint (M), pepper (M) to taste, water (Wa), parsley (Wo), chopped tomatoes (Wo), lemon juice (Wo) to taste, and the grated lemon zest (Wo), and simmer for 12 minutes. Turn off the stove and let the mixture stand for 5 minutes.

STIR in the buttermilk (Wo), paprika (F), and olive oil (E). Season to taste with pepper (M) and transfer to a serving platter. Season to taste with salt (Wa), and garnish with the reserved mint leaves (M) and parsley leaves (Wo).

Caramelized Turnips

Yield: 4 portions

28 ounces small turnips

2 bunches fresh chives

2 tablespoons fresh marjoram

2 onions

2 tablespoons unsalted butter

3 tablespoons sugar

Freshly ground white pepper

2 cups chicken stock

1 tablespoon balsamic vinegar

Dash of mild curry powder

1 tablespoon Dijon mustard

Sea salt

Sliced fresh bread or boiled potatoes

with skins for accompaniment

PREPARATION TIME: 50 MINUTES

relaxes and humidifies from inside

WASH, peel, and quarter the turnips. Wash, spin-dry, and finely chop the chives and fresh marjoram. Peel and dice the onions. Put a large pot over medium heat (F) and add the butter (E). Add 2 tablespoons of the sugar and cook, stirring, until the sugar turns light brown; take care that it doesn't get too dark.

ADD the turnips (M) and sauté for 3-4 minutes, then remove from the pot. Add the diced onions (M) to the pot, season with pepper (M), and sauté until softened. Return the turnips to the pot. Add 1/4 to 1/2 cup of the stock (Wa) at a time and simmer, stirring, until the turnips are done (depending on the type, it will take 12-15 minutes). You may not need to use all of the stock; the turnips should be only lightly covered with sauce.

REMOVE the pot from the heat and stir in the balsamic vinegar (Wo), marjoram (F), remaining 1 tablespoon sugar (E), the chives (M), curry powder (M), mustard (M), and sea salt (Wa) to taste. Serve with bread, or potatoes boiled in their jackets.

Sautéed Chicken with Stuffed Kohlrabi

benefits the lungs

Yield: 4 portions

2 bunches fresh chives • 1 bunch fresh cilantro

1 bunch fresh Italian parsley • 2 stalks lemon grass

4 shallots • 2 cloves garlic

2 tablespoons olive oil

4 boneless, skinless chicken breast halves

2 tablespoons ground white pepper

1/2 cup light soy sauce

1 tablespoon fenugreek seeds

2 carrots • 2 small cucumbers

4 kohlrabi bulbs with leaves

2 cups chicken stock

2 tablespoons crème fraîche

1 teaspoon paprika

2 tablespoons heavy cream

2 tablespoons unsalted butter

Sea salt

**PREPARATION TIME: 2 HOURS,
PLUS 12 HOURS MARINATING TIME**

WASH, dry, and chop the herbs and lemon grass. Peel and mince the shallots and garlic. Put the olive oil (E) in a glass bowl and add the shallots and garlic (M). Rinse the chicken breasts (M), cut them into strips, and add them to the bowl. Add the chives (M), cilantro (M), parsley (Wo), lemon grass (M), pepper (M), soy sauce (Wa), and fenugreek (F), and toss to coat the chicken. Cover and marinate the chicken in the refrigerator for 12 hours, turning several times.

WASH and peel the carrots, cucumbers, and kohlrabi. Finely chop the kohlrabi leaves and hollow out the kohlrabi bulbs with a sharp spoon. Chop the removed kohlrabi flesh. Chop the carrots and 1 1/2 cucumbers.

PREHEAT the oven to 150°F. In a saucepan, heat the stock (Wa) until simmering, and stir in the crème fraîche (Wo). Add the cucumbers, simmer for 3 minutes, and remove from the pan. Add the paprika (F), cream (E), and carrots (E), simmer for 3-4 minutes, and remove the carrots. Add the kohlrabi bulbs (M), simmer for 12 minutes, remove, and keep warm in the oven. Add the chopped kohlrabi to the pan and simmer for 3 minutes.

PLACE a skillet over medium heat (F) and add the butter. Remove the chicken from the marinade, add it to the pan, and sauté, turning to brown both sides. Add the chopped kohlrabi and the cooking liquid, (Wa), cucumbers (Wo), chicken marinade (F) (remove the lemon grass), and carrots (E), and simmer the mixture until the volume is reduced slightly and the chicken is cooked through. Season to taste with pepper (M). Stuff the kohlrabi with the vegetable mixture and season with salt (Wa). Serve with the chicken.

Marinated Daikon Radishes

Yield: 4 portions

2 daikon radishes

Sea salt

1 bunch fresh chives

1 bunch fresh Italian parsley

2 teaspoons flaxseed

1/2 cup olive oil

12 coriander seeds

1 tablespoon mustard seeds

Freshly ground black pepper

2 tablespoons sesame seeds

2 tablespoons pumpkin seeds

2 tablespoons water

1/4 cup fresh lemon juice

1 bunch fresh dill

Dash of paprika

PREPARATION TIME: 45 MINUTES

provides body fluids

PEEL the daikon radishes (M), slice very thinly (preferably with a vegetable slicer or mandoline), and put in a bowl. Sprinkle the radishes with sea salt (Wa), mix well, and let stand for 5 minutes. Carefully press out the juice and arrange the slices on 4 plates, in a circle. Wash, spin-dry, and chop the chives.

WASH, spin-dry, and finely chop the parsley, then sprinkle over the radishes. Sprinkle with the flaxseed (F), and drizzle with the olive oil (E). Mix together the coriander seeds (M), chives (M), mustard seeds (M), a dash of pepper (M), the sesame seeds (Wa), pumpkin seeds (Wa), water (Wa), and lemon juice (Wo), and pour over the radishes. Let the radishes stand for another 10 minutes.

WASH, spin-dry, and finely chop the dill. Sprinkle the radish slices with the paprika (F), dill (E), a dash of ground pepper (M), and salt (Wa) to taste.

Nasi Goreng

Yield: 4 portions

1 bunch celery

1 bunch fresh cilantro

4 large carrots

2 cucumbers

1 tablespoon unsalted butter

4 eggs

Peanut oil for frying

1 package dried shrimp crackers (kroepoek)

1 cup long-grain rice

2 ounces dried shrimp

1 2/3 cups water

Dash of paprika

Sea salt

Juice of 2 lemons

1 teaspoon sugar

Sambal oelek or other hot chile paste

Ketjap manis (Indonesian sweet soy sauce)

PREPARATION TIME: 1 1/2 HOURS

strengthens the immune system

PREHEAT the oven to 150°F. Remove the celery and cilantro leaves, then wash, and finely chop them. Reserve the celery stalks for another use. Peel the carrots and cucumbers and cut them into very thin slices. Put a skillet over medium-high heat (F), add the butter (E) to it, and fry the eggs until cooked to your preference (E). Keep warm in the oven.

POUR a little oil (E) into the skillet and fry two kroepoek (E) at a time until browned on both sides. Transfer to a plate and keep warm in the oven. Repeat until all the kroepoek are fried. Wipe out the skillet with paper towels.

PICK through the rice (E), discarding any grains that are blemished, add it to the skillet, and toast, stirring, for 5 minutes. Add the cilantro leaves (M) and the dried shrimp (Wa) and sauté for 3 minutes. Pour in the water (Wa). Add the celery leaves (Wo) and a dash of paprika (F) and simmer, covered, for 12-15 minutes, until the liquid is absorbed.

PUT some sea salt (Wa) in a bowl and carefully press the cucumber slices (Wo) into the salt. Pour off the resulting liquid. Add the lemon juice (Wo), a dash of paprika (F), carrots (E), and sugar (E) and mix well.

ON each of 4 plates, arrange the vegetable mixture around the edges, and spoon the rice in the middle. Put the fried egg (E) on top of the rice and serve with the fried kroepoek (E). Pass the sambal oelek (M) and sweet soy sauce (Wa), so that each person can season his or her own portion at the table.

Celery Root Puree

Yield: 4 portions

1 small celery root with leaves

2 1/4 pounds baking potatoes

2 onions

1 clove garlic

1 bay leaf

2 1/2 cups water

1 tablespoon white wine vinegar

Small piece of organic lemon zest

4 juniper berries

1/4 cup unsalted butter

1 cup heavy cream

Freshly ground black pepper

Sea salt

PREPARATION TIME: 50 MINUTES

enhances body fluids and energy

TRIM the celery root, cut off the leaves, wash the root carefully, and peel it. Dice the celery root and wash and slice the leaves. Wash, peel, and dice the potatoes.

PEEL and dice the onions and the garlic. In a pot, add the potatoes (E), celery root (M), bay leaf (M), onions (M), garlic (M), water (Wa), vinegar (Wo), lemon zest (Wo), celery root leaves (Wo), and juniper berries (F). Bring just to a boil, reduce to a simmer, and cook until very soft, about 20-25 minutes.

STIR in the butter (E) and cream (E). By hand or with a mixer, puree the ingredients until smooth; take care not to overwork the mixture or it will become gummy. Season the puree to taste with pepper (M) and sea salt (Wa).

Stewed Leeks and Endive with Peanuts

Yield: 4 portions

2 leeks

Sea salt

6 tablespoons white wine vinegar

1 bunch fresh Italian parsley

2 heads Belgian endive

1 tablespoon unsalted butter

1/2 cup short-grain rice

1 piece red or green chile (depending on desired degree of spiciness)

8 ounces roasted, unsalted peanuts

Dash of curry powder

8 coriander seeds

1 cup water

2 tablespoons olive oil

PREPARATION TIME: 40 MINUTES

strengthens your metal element

TRIM and halve the leeks, then thoroughly wash them, and slice them on the diagonal into half-rings. Wash the leeks again and drain well. Put the leeks in a bowl, sprinkle generously with sea salt (Wa), and squeeze the leeks with your hands until they give off their juice. Pour off the juice and add the vinegar (Wo).

PREHEAT the oven to 150°F. Wash, spin-dry, and chop the parsley. Trim and halve the endive (F). Set a skillet over medium heat (F) and add the unsalted butter (E). Add the endive halves and sauté for 3-4 minutes on each side. Remove and keep warm in the oven.

PICK through the rice (E), discarding any grains that are blemished, add it to a saucepan, and toast, stirring, for 5 minutes. Wash, trim, seed, and chop the chile. Squeeze the liquid from the leeks and put them in the pan with the rice. Add the peanuts (M), curry powder (M), chile (M), coriander seeds (M), water (Wa), and parsley (Wo). Cover the pot and simmer the mixture for 10-15 minutes, until the rice has absorbed the liquid and the vegetables are tender. Serve the leek-rice mixture on plates topped with the endive halves (F) and drizzled with the olive oil (E).

Duck in Star Anise Sauce

Yield: 6 portions

2 sprigs fresh thyme

1 bunch fresh basil

1 bunch fresh Italian parsley

8 carrots

4 stalks celery

2 organic oranges

4 cloves garlic

4 shallots

10 ounces snow peas

2 ducks, about 3 pounds each

1/4 cup unsalted butter

Freshly ground black pepper

4 pods star anise

2 tablespoons mustard seeds

1/4 cup Grand Marnier (or other orange liqueur)

2 tablespoons sugar

Sea salt

PREPARATION TIME: 1 HOUR, PLUS 15 MINUTES RESTING TIME

warms you up on cold days

THOROUGHLY wash, spin-dry, and finely chop the herbs. Peel the carrots and celery and cut them in half; reserve the peels. Wash the oranges, grate the zest, and squeeze the juice. Peel the garlic and shallots, wash the snow peas, and trim the ends.

WASH the ducks and pat them dry with paper towels. Remove the breasts and drumsticks. Place the duck carcasses in a pot with the vegetable peels and just cover with water. Bring to a boil and reduce to a simmer.

PREHEAT the oven to 150°F. Melt the butter (E) in a large skillet over medium heat, and sauté the halved vegetables (E) for 4 minutes on each side; remove the vegetables from the skillet. Season the duck pieces with pepper (M). Add the drumsticks to the skillet and sauté for 10 minutes without turning. Add the thyme (M), garlic (M), shallots (M), star anise (M), mustard seeds (M), and the duck breasts (skin-side down) and turn the drumsticks. Sauté over high heat for 10-12 minutes, turning the breasts and drumsticks once, and remove from the skillet. Keep warm in the oven.

STRAIN the stock made from the duck bones (Wa) into the skillet and cook it down a little. Add the orange juice (Wo), parsley (Wo), basil (F), orange zest (E), Grand Marnier (E), sugar (E), snow peas (E), carrots, and celery (E) and simmer for 10 minutes. Season to taste with pepper (M). Serve the duck pieces over the vegetables and season to taste with salt (Wa).

Quail with Pumpkin Seed Fritters

Yield: 4 portions

8 ounces dried garbanzo beans

1 bunch fresh Italian parsley

1 bunch fresh basil

2 egg yolks

1 teaspoon turmeric

1 teaspoon ground coriander

6 cloves garlic • Sea salt

1/4 cup chopped pumpkin seeds

1 teaspoon paprika

2 tablespoons flour

1/4 cup sunflower oil

4 quails

2 shallots

12 black peppercorns

1 bunch fresh thyme

2 tablespoons unsalted butter

2 bunches green onions

Freshly ground black pepper

PREPARATION TIME: 1 1/2 HOURS, PLUS 8 HOURS SOAKING TIME

SOAK the garbanzo beans (Wa) overnight in a large amount of water (Wa). Pour off the water and add fresh water to cover the beans in a pot.

strengthens lungs and kidneys

Wash the parsley (Wo) and basil (F), and add a few sprigs of each to the pot. Chop the remaining herbs. Put the pot on the stove (F), bring just to a boil, then turn down the heat, and simmer until the beans are tender, about 45 minutes.

WITH a hand blender, puree the garbanzos with their cooking liquid. Stir in the egg yolks (E), turmeric, and coriander (M). Peel and mince the garlic (M) and add 2/3 of it to the pot. Season to taste with salt (Wa), add the pumpkin seeds (Wa), parsley (Wo), basil (F), and paprika (F), and puree again. Stir in the flour (E). Let the entire mixture rest, covered, for 30 minutes.

PREHEAT the oven to 150°F. Form the bean mixture into small balls. Heat the sunflower oil (E) in a skillet over medium-high to high heat, and fry the balls in the oil until crisp. Drain the fritters on paper towels and keep warm in the oven. Pour out the oil and wipe the skillet clean.

RINSE the quails (M) and pat them dry with paper towels. Stuff them with the peeled shallots (M), the remaining garlic (M), the peppercorns (M), and washed thyme, dividing evenly. Melt the butter (E) in the skillet over medium-high heat. Add the quails and sauté on each side for 7-8 minutes. Trim and wash the green onions (M), slice them on the diagonal, add to the skillet, and sauté until tender. Serve the quail and onions with the fritters, seasoned to taste with pepper (M) and sea salt (Wa).

Stuffed Breast of Chicken

provides new energy

Yield: 4 portions

1 small head cauliflower

4 boneless free-range chicken breasts with the skin

Freshly ground black pepper

4 ounces Gorgonzola cheese

Grated zest of 1 organic lemon

Paprika

1/4 cup prepared pesto

3/4 cup millet

2-3 sprigs fresh thyme

2 tablespoons unsalted butter

4 onions

1 1/4 cups water

1 tablespoon olive oil

Sea salt

In addition:

4 wooden toothpicks, soaked in oil

PREPARATION TIME: 1 HOUR, 10 MINUTES

SEPARATE the cauliflower into florets, wash them, and cut each in half. Wash the chicken breasts (M), pat them dry, and cut a pocket into each one on the thicker end. Season the inside of each pocket with pepper (M), and insert a 1-ounce piece of Gorgonzola (M/Wa).

DIVIDE a small amount of lemon zest (Wo), a dash of paprika (F) and pesto (F) among the pockets. Close each breast pocket securely with a toothpick.

SORT through the millet to remove any odd-looking pieces. Wash the thyme and pull off the leaves. Place a large skillet over medium-high heat (F), add the millet (E), and toast for 10 minutes, stirring frequently; remove from the heat. Melt the butter in the skillet, add the cauliflower florets (E), and sauté over high heat until the florets start to brown. Transfer the mixture to a plate and sprinkle with the fresh thyme leaves (M).

PREHEAT the oven to 150°F. Lay the chicken breasts (M) in the skillet, skin-side down, and sauté over medium-high heat for 12-15 minutes, until crisp and golden; turn over, and cook for another 10 minutes. Remove from the skillet and keep warm in the oven.

PEEL the onions (M), chop them, and sauté them in the skillet until translucent. Return the millet-cauliflower mixture to the skillet. Add the water (Wa), remaining lemon zest (Wo), and a dash of paprika (F), and simmer for 15 minutes. Turn off the stove and let the millet stand for 10 minutes. Stir in the olive oil (E) and pepper (M) to taste. Serve the chicken breasts over the millet and sprinkle with sea salt (Wa) to taste.

Crispy Fried Chicken Wings

Yield: 4 portions

24 chicken wings, small ends removed

8 cloves garlic

1 organic lemon

2 bunches fresh basil

Curry powder

6 tablespoons light soy sauce

2 tablespoons light sesame oil

2 tablespoons unsalted butter, plus more if needed

1 cup flour

Sea salt

PREPARATION TIME: 1 HOUR, PLUS 4 HOURS MARINATING TIME

nourishes your metal element

WASH the chicken wings (M), pat them dry, and place them in a large bowl. Peel the garlic (M), slice it finely, and add it to the bowl. Wash the lemon and grate the zest. Wash, spin-dry, and finely chop the basil.

IN a bowl, mix together a dash of curry powder (M), the soy sauce (Wa), sesame oil (Wo), lemon zest (Wo), and basil (F), pour the mixture over the chicken wings, and mix well to coat the wings with the marinade. Cover the bowl and refrigerate for 4 hours, turning occasionally. Drain the wings before cooking, reserving the marinade.

PLACE a large skillet over medium heat (F) and melt the butter (E). Add the chicken wings (M) and sauté until they're browned and almost cooked through, about 5 minutes on each side. Let the wings cool, and then pull the bones out of the wings.

PUT the flour (E) on a plate, sprinkle with a pinch of curry powder (M), and mix well. Coat the chicken wings with the flour mixture, shaking off the excess. Return the skillet to medium heat, adding more butter if necessary, and sauté the coated chicken wings until crisp and brown on both sides; remove from the skillet. Add the reserved marinade (Wa) to the pan, and let it cook down a little, stirring well. Use the reduced marinade as a dipping sauce with the fried wings. Season the wings to taste with sea salt (Wa).

Artichokes with Blue Cheese Dip

Yield: 4 portions

1 bunch fresh Italian parsley

Zest and juice of 1 organic lemon

4 artichokes

2 tablespoons olive oil

1/4 cup heavy cream

Freshly ground black pepper

8 ounces Roquefort cheese

Sea salt

1/4 cup crème fraîche

Paprika

PREPARATION TIME: 30 MINUTES

regenerates and tonifies

WASH, spin-dry, and finely chop the parsley. Put 2 quarts water (Wa) in a pot, add the lemon zest (Wo) and a splash of the juice (Wo), and bring to a boil.

CUT the stem off each artichoke (F) and remove the pointy tips of the leaves. Boil the artichokes for 30-45 minutes, until the base is tender; drain and cool.

IN a bowl, mix the olive oil (E), cream (E), pepper (M), crumbled Roquefort cheese (M/Wa), salt (Wa) to taste, crème fraîche (Wo), lemon juice (Wo) to taste, and a dash of paprika (F) into a thick dip. Serve with the cooked artichokes.

Fragrant Sunday Rice

provides moisture for the lungs

Yield: 4 portions

1 cup basmati rice

2 zucchini

2 bunches green onions

1 sprig fresh thyme

1 organic lemon

4 juniper berries

1 teaspoon fennel seeds

1 teaspoon curry powder

8 coriander seeds

1 teaspoon black cardamom seeds

2 cups water

2 tablespoons unsalted butter

Freshly ground black pepper

Sea salt

PREPARATION TIME: 45 MINUTES

PICK through the rice and discard any grains that are blemished. Wash and trim the zucchini and cut them in strips. Trim and wash the green onions, and slice them on the diagonal. Wash and spin-dry the thyme and pluck off the leaves. Wash the lemon, grate the zest, and squeeze the juice.

PUT a saucepan over medium heat (F), and add 2 of the juniper berries (F). Add the fennel seeds (E), rice (M), curry powder (M), coriander (M), cardamom (M), and thyme (M) leaves, and toast everything for 4 minutes, stirring occasionally.

ADD the green onions (M) to the saucepan and pour in the water (Wa). Add the remaining 2 juniper berries (F) and the zucchini (E), cover the pan, and simmer the rice for 12-15 minutes, until all of the liquid is absorbed. Remove the pan from the heat and let the rice stand for 5 minutes. Stir in the butter (E), then season to taste with pepper (M), salt (Wa), and lemon juice.

WATER ELEMENT

WINTER — gathering forces for a new beginning. The recipes of this element nourish and strengthen your vital energy, for water, after all, is the source of all life. We come from water, and we consist in large part of water (80%). After a long illness, a period of heightened stress, or interval of great exhaustion, your water element lacks energy; you feel empty. One to two servings of fish per week will give you back your strength. Add salt to foods only after cooking. This will give you greater flavor with smaller amounts of salt.

Cook foods from the water element if you:

- feel cold and low in energy
- often feel anxious
- frequently have problems in the urinary tract
- suffer from bone disease
- want to take special care of yourself in the winter

Calamari Salad with Zucchini and Carrots

feeds the body's juices

Yield: 4 portions

2 pounds squid bodies

Freshly ground black pepper

1 stalk lemon grass

2 cups water

1 organic lemon

2 bunches fresh Italian parsley

Paprika

2 tomatoes

2 onions

2 large carrots

2 zucchini

4-6 tablespoons olive oil

Sea salt

PREPARATION TIME: 1 HOUR, PLUS 30 MINUTES MARINATING TIME

CUT the squid into 3/4-inch pieces. Put a few grindings of pepper (M) in a saucepan. Wash the lemon grass, cut it into rings, and add it to the pot (M). Pour in the water (Wa) and add the squid pieces (Wa). Wash the lemon, and grate the zest or strip it off with a zester. Squeeze the lemon juice. Add the lemon juice (Wo) and zest (Wo) to the pan. Wash the parsley (Wo), add the stems to the pan, and chop the leaves.

PUT the pan on the stove (F), and bring the water just to a boil, then quickly reduce to a simmer. Simmer the squid for 3 minutes (no longer, otherwise it will get tough). Remove the pan from the heat. Drain the squid, reserving the cooking liquid. Put the squid in a bowl, sprinkle lightly with paprika (F), and let cool.

WASH the tomatoes, and peel if desired. Remove the stems and chop the tomato flesh. Peel and dice the onions. Season the squid-cooking water with paprika (F). Peel the carrots (E) and cut into fine slices. Wash the zucchini (E) and cut into strips. Add the carrots and zucchini to the pot and simmer for a few minutes, until tender-crisp. Add the vegetables to the bowl with the squid. Add the onions (M) to the pan, and simmer until the stock is cooked down to about 2 cups.

POUR the oil (E) over the squid, season to taste with pepper (M) and salt (Wa), and add the stock (Wa). Stir in the tomatoes (Wo) and parsley (Wo) and let the salad marinate for 30 minutes before serving.

146

Adzuki Bean Salad with Smoked Salmon

Yield: 4 portions

8 ounces adzuki beans or small white beans

2 onions

1 bunch fresh Italian parsley

1 organic lemon

1 bay leaf

Dash of paprika

2 tablespoons olive oil

Freshly ground black pepper

Sea salt

1/4 cup light sesame oil

12 slices smoked salmon

PREPARATION TIME: 45 MINUTES, PLUS 12 HOURS SOAKING TIME

strengthens the water element

PICK through the beans, discarding any that are blemished, and soak them overnight in a large amount of water. Peel and dice the onions. Wash, spin-dry, and finely chop the parsley. Wash the lemon, grate the zest, and squeeze the juice.

IN a large saucepan, add the bay leaf (M), onions (M), drained soaked beans (Wa), enough water to cover everything (Wa), lemon zest and juice (Wo), and parsley (H) and place over high heat (F). Add a dash of paprika (F) and bring to a boil. Reduce the heat so that the mixture simmers, cover the pan, and cook the beans until tender, about 25 minutes.

DRAIN the beans, pouring the cooking liquid into a saucepan. Cook down the bean cooking liquid a little. Put the beans in a bowl and add the olive oil (E), pepper (M) to taste, a little of the cooking liquid (Wa), and sea salt (Wa) to taste, and let stand briefly.

JUST before serving, divide the bean salad among serving plates and drizzle with the sesame oil (Wo). Arrange the smoked salmon (Wa) on the plates.

Chestnut Puree with Cabbage

Yield: 4 portions

10 ounces whole fresh chestnuts

2 1/4 pounds baking potatoes

1 bunch fresh Italian parsley

1 small head green cabbage

2 onions

Freshly ground black pepper

Dash of nutmeg

1 quart water

2 tablespoons fresh lemon juice

4 juniper berries

6 tablespoons unsalted butter

1 cup heavy cream

Sea salt

2 tablespoons sesame seeds

2 tablespoons sour cream

Pinch of paprika

PREPARATION TIME: 1 1/4 HOURS

PREHEAT the oven to 400°F. At the pointed ends, score the chestnut peels in an X shape. Spread the scored chestnuts on a baking sheet, and roast in the oven for 20-25 minutes. Remove the chestnut peels with a paring knife.

new strength for the water element

WASH, peel, and quarter the baking potatoes. Wash, spin-dry, and chop the parsley. Quarter the cabbage, cut out the core, wash the cabbage, and cut it into fine strips. Peel and dice the onions.

PREHEAT the oven to 150°F. Put a large saucepan on the stove (F), and add the potatoes (E), peeled chestnuts (E), onions (M), pepper (M) and grated nutmeg (M) to taste, water (Wa), lemon juice (Wo), and juniper berries (F). Bring just to a boil, then reduce to a simmer, and cook, covered, for 20 minutes, until the potatoes are tender. Drain, pouring the cooking liquid into another pan, and let it cook down. Put the potato mixture into a bowl and add 4 tablespoons of the butter (E), 2/3 cup of the cream (E), and pepper (M) and salt (Wa) to taste. Puree the mixture by hand or with a mixer, taking care not to overwork the puree or it will become gummy. Gradually work in 1/2 cup of the reduced cooking liquid, and keep the puree warm in the oven.

PUT a skillet over medium heat (F), add the remaining 2 tablespoons butter (E) and 1/3 cup cream (E), pepper (M) to taste, and the cabbage (Wa), and simmer for 15 minutes, until the cabbage is tender. Remove the skillet from the heat and season the cabbage to taste with sea salt (Wa). Sprinkle the sesame seeds (Wa) over the cabbage, stir in the sour cream (Wo), and sprinkle with the paprika (F). Serve with the chestnut puree.

Miso Soup

Yield: 4 portions

1 quart water

Piece of organic lemon zest

2 green onions

2 ounces yellow miso paste

PREPARATION TIME: 15 MINUTES

strengthens the water element

PUT the water (Wa) in a saucepan, add the lemon zest (Wo), and bring to a boil. (F).

WASH and trim the green onions (M), cut them on the diagonal into very fine rings, and distribute among 4 soup bowls. Divide the miso paste (Wa) among the bowls, add a little warm water, and stir until smooth. Divide the boiling lemon water among the bowls, stir, and serve.

Carrot Salad with Oranges

Yield: 4 portions

8 carrots

8 organic oranges

1/4 cup lemon juice

Dash of freshly grated nutmeg

1/2 tablespoon raw (turbinado) sugar

2 tablespoons green peppercorns

Sea salt

PREPARATION TIME: 1 HOUR

good for kidneys, spleen, and liver

PEEL and shred the carrots. Wash the oranges, and grate the zest of one. Peel and fillet the oranges (Wo) (see page 80 for instructions on filleting citrus) and place the orange fillets in a bowl (drink any collected orange juice, or reserve for another use). Add the lemon juice (Wo) to the bowl.

PUT the nutmeg in a saucepan. Add the sugar (E), lemon zest (E), and carrots (E) and steam the carrots for 3 minutes. Cool and transfer the carrot mixture to the bowl with the orange fillets. Add the green peppercorns (M), and season to taste with sea salt (Wa).

Mussel Soup with Barley Sprouts

builds up yin

Yield: 4 portions

3 ounces hulled barley

2 carrots • 1/4 celery root

1 leek

1 bunch fresh Italian parsley

5 pounds fresh mussels in their shells

1 quart water

2/3 cup dry Riesling, or other white wine

8 juniper berries

2 onions

2 tablespoons unsalted butter

2 tablespoons flour

2 bay leaves

Freshly ground black pepper

1 quart fish stock

Sea salt

2 tablespoons crème fraîche

Dash of paprika

PREPARATION TIME: 1 1/2 HOURS, PLUS 3-4 DAYS SPROUTING TIME

THREE to four days before serving, soak the barley in water, put in a covered container, and set on the countertop. Rinse the barley 3 times daily with fresh water. After 3-4 days, the grain will form sprouts.

WASH and trim the carrots, celery root, and leek, then chop. Wash and spin-dry the parsley. With a brush, scrub the mussels (Wa) well under running water, removing the hairy filaments attached to the shells (beards), and throwing away any that are open. Place the mussels in a pot. Pour in the water (Wa), wine (Wa), a few parsley stems (Wo), and the juniper berries (F), and place over medium-high heat (F). Cover the pot and steam the mussels until all most of them have opened, about 6 minutes. (Discard any mussels that refuse to open). Take the mussels out of the pot and remove them from the shells. Pour the cooking liquid through a very fine sieve.

PEEL and mince the onions. Finely chop the remaining parsley. Put a saucepan over medium heat (F), and add the butter (E). Add the carrots (E) and sauté for a few minutes. Add the flour (E), onions (M), the celery root (M), leek (M), and bay leaves (M), cover, and simmer for 6-7 minutes. Season to taste with pepper (M). Add the fish stock (Wa) and the mussel cooking liquid (Wa), and simmer for 15 minutes.

ADD the shelled mussels (Wa) to the pot and pour the soup into a serving container. Sprinkle the soup with the barley sprouts (Wa) and season to taste with salt (Wa). Garnish with the crème fraîche (Wo), chopped parsley (Wo), and paprika.

Seafood Omelet

Yield: 4 portions

8 ounces sole fillets, or other mild white fish fillets

8 fresh eggs

4 ounces cherry tomatoes

1 zucchini

1 bunch fresh Italian parsley

1 onion

2 tablespoons unsalted butter

Freshly ground black pepper

Pinch of curry powder

6 ounces peeled shrimp or crayfish meat

Dash of paprika

Sea salt

PREPARATION TIME: 35 MINUTES

nourishes kidneys and bladder

RINSE the fish fillets and cut them into 2-inch pieces. Blend the eggs carefully in a bowl (without beating them). Wash and halve the cherry tomatoes, and remove the stems. Wash and trim the zucchini, slice it once lengthwise, and then cut it crosswise into strips. Wash, spin-dry, and mince the parsley. Peel and mince the onion. Preheat the oven to 350°F.

PUT an ovenproof skillet over medium heat (F). Add 1 1/2 tablespoons of the butter (E) and let it melt. Pour in the eggs (E), then add the zucchini strips (E). Sprinkle with pepper (M) to taste, the minced onion (M), and pinch of curry powder (M).

PLACE the fish fillets (Wa), shrimp or crayfish (Wa/Wo), parsley (Wo), and tomatoes (Wo) on top and sprinkle with the paprika (F). Put the skillet in the oven and bake the omelet for 10-12 minutes, until it has doubled in volume.

QUICKLY distribute the remaining 1/2 tablespoon of the butter (E) in little pieces over the omelet, season to taste with pepper (M) and sea salt (Wa), and serve immediately, cut into wedges.

Soybeans with Red Peppers

refreshes and invigorates

Yield: 4 portions

4 ounces shelled soybeans

18 ounces fresh broad green beans

2 red bell peppers

2 carrots

1 onion

1/4 cup buckwheat groats

2 tablespoons unsalted butter

1 bay leaf

Freshly ground black pepper

1 organic lemon

2 tablespoons balsamic vinegar

A dash of paprika

2 tablespoons olive oil

Sea salt

PREPARATION TIME: 2 HOUR, PLUS 12 HOURS SOAKING TIME.

PICK through the soybeans and discard any that are blemished. Soak the beans, covered with water, overnight.

WASH the green beans, red pepper, and carrots. Slice the beans on the diagonal. Halve, core, and dice the red peppers. Peel the carrots, slice them once lengthwise, and then cut crosswise into strips. Peel and dice the onion.

PUT a pot on the stove over medium heat (F) and toast the buckwheat (F) and the carrot strips (E) for 7-8 minutes, stirring occasionally; then transfer the mixture to a bowl. Add 1 tablespoon of the butter (E) and diced peppers (F) to the pot, and sauté for 2 minutes. Remove the mixture from the pot and add it to the bowl with the buckwheat.

IN a large saucepan, sauté the diced onion (M) in the remaining 1 tablespoon butter until translucent. Add the bay leaf (F), season to taste with pepper (M), and then add the drained soybeans (Wa). Cover the ingredients with water (Wa) and bring to a boil. Wash the lemon, cut off the zest, and squeeze the juice. Add the lemon zest and juice (Wo), vinegar (Wo), and green beans (Wo) to the saucepan. Sprinkle with the paprika (F) and simmer, covered, for 10 minutes. Add the buckwheat-vegetable mixture, and simmer for another 20 minutes. Drizzle with the olive oil (E), and season to taste with pepper (M) and sea salt (Wa) before serving.

Noodles with Sprouted Garbanzo Beans

Yield: 4 portions

4 ounces dried garbanzo beans

4 carrots

4 tomatoes

1 bunch fresh Italian parsley

2 bunches fresh chives

1 organic lemon

1 organic orange

2 onions

1 bunch green onions

Paprika

1 pound dried tagliatelle (thin noodles)

Freshly ground black pepper

Sea salt

6 tablespoons sour cream

Dash of freshly grated nutmeg

PREPARATION TIME: 1 1/2 HOURS, PLUS 2 DAYS SPROUTING TIME

strengthens the kidneys and bladder

COVER the garbanzo beans with water and soak overnight. Pour off the water, cover, and set aside for about 2 days, until the beans sprout; rinse the beans every 6-8 hours with lukewarm water.

WASH, peel or trim, and chop the carrots, tomatoes, parsley, and chives. Grate the zests of the lemon and the orange, or strip them off with a zester. Squeeze the lemon juice and set it aside. Peel and chop the onions. Trim, wash, and chop the green onions.

FILL two pots with 1 quart each of water (Wa), and put the sprouted garbanzo beans (Wa) in one pot. Divide the lemon juice (H) and a dash of paprika (F) between the pots, and bring the water to a boil. When the water is boiling, add the noodles (E) to the second pot, followed by the carrots (E), onions (M), and green onions (M), and cook until the pasta is slightly firm to the bite (al dente), according to the directions on the package. Simmer the garbanzo beans for about 10 minutes. Drain the noodle-vegetable mixture, place in a large bowl, and sprinkle with freshly ground pepper (M) to taste, and the chives (M).

DRAIN the garbanzo beans and add them to the bowl. Season to taste with salt (Wa), then mix in the lemon zest (Wo), orange zest (E), sour cream (Wo), parsley (Wo), tomatoes (Wo), nutmeg (F), and a dash of paprika (F); mix well and serve.

Smoked Trout with Potatoes Two Ways

supports your water element

Yield: 4 portions

2 onions

2 cloves garlic

1 bunch fresh Italian parsley

1 organic lemon

2 cucumbers

4 large baking potatoes

1 pound small boiling potatoes

1 bay leaf

Sea salt

Dash of paprika

Freshly ground black pepper

8 ounces smoked trout

5 tablespoons unsalted butter

2 tablespoons water

4 tablespoons crème fraîche

8 coriander seeds

PREPARATION TIME: 1 HOUR

PEEL and dice the onions and garlic. Wash, spin-dry, and finely chop the parsley. Wash the lemon, grate the zest, and squeeze the juice. Peel the cucumbers and cut into small dice. Wash both types of potatoes, and peel the baking potatoes.

PREHEAT the oven to 150°F. Put the boiling potatoes (E) in a saucepan. Add the garlic (M) and bay leaf (M), cover with water (Wa), and bring to a boil. Add a dash of salt (Wa), a little of the lemon juice (Wo), and a dash of paprika (F), reduce the heat, and simmer the potatoes until tender, about 20 minutes. Drain the potatoes and keep them warm in the oven. Shred the baking potatoes (E) with a cheese grater, press out their juices, and put them in a bowl; season to taste with pepper (M) and sea salt (Wa).

CUT the trout (Wa) into pieces and put into the bowl with the grated potatoes. Add the grated lemon zest (Wo), a dash of paprika (F), and 1 tablespoon of the butter (E), and mix well. Place a heavy cast-iron skillet over medium-high heat (F), and add 3 tablespoons of the butter (E). Add the potato (E) and trout (W) mixture to the pan and press down evenly. Cook until the crust is golden brown, then carefully flip the potato "pancake," and brown the other side. Season with pepper (M) to taste and keep warm in the oven.

ADD the onion to the skillet and sauté until translucent. Add the water (Wa) and lemon juice (Wo) and stir well. Add the diced cucumbers (Wo), crème fraîche (Wo), coriander (F), parsley (E), the remaining 1 tablespoon butter (E), and pepper (M) to taste, and cook everything down to a smooth sauce. Serve the sauce to accompany the trout in the potato crust and the boiled potatoes. Season to taste with sea salt (Wa).

Sushi with Sole and Cucumber

Yield: 4 portions

moistens the water and metal elements

1 bunch arugula

1 English (seedless) cucumber

1 carrot • 1 bunch green onions

18 ounces sole (ask the fishmonger
to fillet it and give you the bones)

2 cups water

Small piece of organic lemon zest

3 fennel seeds

1 cup sushi rice or sticky rice

Freshly ground white pepper

1 tablespoon flour

1 tablespoon unsalted butter

Sea salt

8 sheets nori (toasted seaweed) • 1/2 cup sesame seeds

3 tablespoons rice vinegar

Wasabi paste • Soy sauce

PREPARATION TIME: 1 1/4 HOURS

TRIM and wash the arugula. Cut off the lower third of the stems. Peel the cucumber and the carrot. Cut the cucumber lengthwise into eighths, and dice. Cut the carrot lengthwise into strips. Trim and wash the green onions; cut off the top third of the green ends. Place the vegetable trimmings, fish bones, water, and lemon zest in a saucepan and bring to a boil. Reduce the heat and simmer the stock until it reduces to about 1 cup.

PLACE a saucepan over medium heat (F), add the fennel seeds (E) and rice (E), and toast, stirring, for 3 minutes. Season to taste with pepper (M) and pour in the reduced stock (Wa). Cover the pot and cook the rice for 12-15 minutes, until it has absorbed all of the liquid. Remove from the heat and let the rice stand for 10 minutes.

QUARTER the fish fillets. Put the flour (E) in a dish and season with pepper (M). Dip the fish pieces in the flour, and shake off the excess. Place a skillet over medium heat (F), and add the butter (E). Add the fish to the skillet and sauté until browned on both sides and cooked through. Season to taste with salt (Wa). Let the fish cool.

SPREAD the nori sheets (Wa) on a work surface, on top of bamboo mats or kitchen towels. Cover the nori sheets with the rice, leaving the front third of the sheets empty. Over the middle thirds, sprinkle the sesame seeds (Wa), and lay two pieces each of cooled fish (Wa). Divide the cucumber (Wo), vinegar (Wo), arugula (F), carrots (E), and green onions (M) over the sesame seeds. Spread the remaining rice surface with a little wasabi (M). With the help of the bamboo mat or kitchen towel, roll up the nori sheet around the rice and filling, and press it firmly into a roll. Slice the rolls crosswise with a very sharp knife, dipping it into cold water between cuts. Serve with dishes of additional wasabi (M) and soy sauce (Wa) at the table.

Sea Bass with Wild Rice

provides moisture

Yield: 4 portions

2 1/4 pounds sea bass or cod fillets

1 cup wild rice

1 cup long-grain rice

2 onions

3 cloves garlic

1 small leek

1 carrot

4 tomatoes

1 bunch arugula

2 tablespoons unsalted butter

3 pods star anise

Freshly ground black pepper

2 cups fish stock

1/4 cup crème fraîche

Dash of paprika

Sea salt

PREPARATION TIME: 50 MINUTES

REMOVE the gray skin from the fish fillets. Pick through both types of rice and remove any grains that are blemished. Peel and dice the onions and garlic. Trim, halve, and wash the leek, then cut it on the diagonal into half-rings. Peel the carrot, slice it once lengthwise, then cut it crosswise into strips. Wash the tomatoes, and remove the peels, if desired. Remove the stems from the tomatoes, and chop. Trim, wash, and chop the arugula.

PREHEAT the oven to 150°F. Place a skillet over medium heat (F), and add 1 1/2 tablespoons of the butter (E), the star anise (M), and garlic (M). Add the sea bass (Wa) and sauté for 5 minutes on each side. Keep the fish warm in the oven.

PUT a saucepan over medium heat (F) and add the carrot. Add the long-grain rice (M), onions (M), pepper (M), leek (M), and wild rice (Wa), and toast for 10 minutes, stirring frequently. Pour in the fish stock (Wa). Stir in the crème fraîche (Wo), tomatoes (Wo), arugula (F), and paprika (F), and simmer, covered, over low heat for 20 minutes.

REMOVE the pan from the heat and let stand for 10 minutes. Stir in the remaining butter (E), and pepper (M) and sea salt (Wa) to taste. Season the fish with sea salt (Wa), cut into diagonal slices, and serve with the rice.

Stuffed Squid

Yield: 4 portions

replenishes depleted juices

1 pound mild white fish fillets

4 large, whole squid bodies (the freshest you can find)

4 cloves garlic • 2 shallots

1 organic lemon

1 bunch Swiss chard

1 cup heavy cream

Freshly ground white pepper • Sea salt

Paprika

2 tablespoons small capers

4 ounces pitted green olives

2 tablespoons unsalted butter

2 cups fish stock

1/4 cup crème fraîche

In addition:

8 wooden toothpicks, soaked in oil • Kitchen string

PREPARATION TIME: 1 HOUR

CUT the fish fillets into pieces and chill. Rinse the squid bodies and pat them dry. Peel and mince the garlic and shallots. Wash the lemon, grate the zest, and squeeze the juice. Trim the chard, wash it, and slice it diagonally.

TO a blender, add 2/3 cup of the cream (E), the garlic (M), pepper (M) to taste, and the chilled fish (Wa); puree until smooth, and season with salt (Wa). Stuff the squid bodies (Wa) with the filling and secure the ends with toothpicks.

PREHEAT the oven to 150°F. Put the chard (Wo) and lemon zest (Wo) in a large skillet or roaster, sprinkle with paprika (F), and place over high heat (F). Add the capers (F), olives (F), and butter (E) and sauté until the chard is slightly wilted. Season to taste with pepper (M), sprinkle with the minced shallots (M), and sauté for a few more minutes. Remove the chard mixture from the skillet and keep warm in the oven.

PLACE the stuffed squid (Wa) in the skillet and sauté for 6 minutes on each side. Pour in the fish stock (Wa), 2 tablespoons of the lemon juice (Wo), the crème fraîche (Wo), and a dash of paprika (F). Cook, covered, for 10 minutes, then remove the squid from the skillet and keep warm in the oven.

SIMMER the cooking liquid until it is reduced to about 3/4 cup. Stir in the remaining 1/3 cup cream (E) and season to taste with pepper (M). Turn off the stove, put the chard and the vegetables back in the stock, and let stand, covered, for 5 minutes. Season to taste with salt (Wa). To serve, divide the chard mixture among serving plates and place the stuffed squid on top.

Turbot with Fennel Gratin

strengthens the kidneys

Yield: 4 portions

4 bulbs fennel

4 carrots

1 bunch fresh Italian parsley

1 organic lemon

2 onions

4 juniper berries

1 bay leaf

Freshly ground pepper

2 cups water • 2 cups fish stock

Paprika

3 tablespoons unsalted butter

1/4 cup crème fraîche

1/4 cup heavy cream

28 ounces turbot, sole, or flounder fillets with the skin

Sea salt

PREPARATION TIME: 1 HOUR, PLUS 15 MINUTES BAKING TIME

TRIM and wash the fennel and carrots, and cut them into slices. Wash, spin-dry, and chop the parsley. Wash the lemon, then remove the zest, and squeeze the juice. Peel and dice the onions. Put 2 juniper berries (F), the fennel (E), and carrots (E) in a saucepan. Add the bay leaf (M), pepper (M) to taste, water, stock (Wa), half of the lemon zest (Wo) and a dash of paprika (F).

Bring the mixture just to a boil, then reduce to a simmer and cook, covered, for 8 minutes. Transfer the chopped vegetables to a flameproof baking dish. Simmer the stock mixture until it is reduced to about 1/2 cup. Preheat the oven to 325°F.

ADD 1 tablespoon butter (E) to the dish with the vegetables, season to taste with pepper (M), and pour in the reduced stock (Wa). Top with the rest of the lemon zest (Wo), the parsley (Wo), crème fraîche (Wo), a dash of paprika (F), and 2 tablespoons of the cream (E). Bake for 15 minutes.

IN each of two skillets, melt 1 tablespoon of the remaining butter (E) over medium heat (F). Divide the diced onions (M) among the skillets, arranging them in a ring around the perimeter; season with pepper (M) and add the fish fillets (Wa) to the skillet with the skin-side down. When the fish looks cooked almost through, with only a narrow glassy-looking strip on the top, place the fish in a warmed serving dish (with the skin down); season to taste with salt (Wa) and cover.

TO the combined juices from both pans, add a little lemon juice (Wo), the remaining 2 juniper berries (F), a dash of paprika (F), and the remaining 2 tablespoons cream; season to taste with pepper (M) and cook the liquid down to a sauce consistency. Season the sauce to taste with salt (W) and pour over the fish. Pull the skin off the fish before serving.

Saddle of Venison with Red Wine Shallots

gives you energy on cold days

Yield: 4 portions

8 ounces small shallots

1 organic orange

4 firm, ripe pears

4 carrots

4 stalks celery

2 cups full-bodied red wine

3 tablespoons sugar

1 cinnamon stick

Freshly ground black pepper

2 tablespoons unsalted butter

2 pods star anise

1 bay leaf

28 ounces saddle of venison (trimmed of tendons and fat)

1 cup veal stock

4 juniper berries

Sea salt

PREPARATION TIME: 1 1/2 HOURS

PEEL the shallots. Wash the orange and grate the zest or strip it off with a zester; squeeze the orange juice. Peel the pears, and cut in half, leaving the stems in tact. Peel the carrots. Cut the carrots and celery in half. Core the pears.

PREHEAT the oven to 150°F. Pour the red wine (F) into a large pot (with a lid) and set over medium-low heat (F). Add the sugar (E), pears (E), orange zest (E), shallots (M), cinnamon stick (M), and pepper to taste, and simmer for 12-15 minutes, until the pears are tender. Remove the pears and keep warm in the oven.

COOK the sauce down so that it clings slightly to the onions, and remove the cinnamon stick. Place a large heavy-bottomed skillet over medium heat (F) and melt the butter (E). Add the carrots (E), celery (E), star anise (M), pepper (M) to taste, and bay leaf (M). Sauté the vegetables for a few minutes, then push to the sides of the pan. Add the venison (M/Wa) to the pan and cook for 10-12 minutes on each side. Remove the venison from the pan and keep warm in the oven. Add the stock (Wa) and orange juice (Wo) to the pan and simmer, stirring. Add the juniper berries (F) and let the mixture cook down to a sauce consistency.

LAY the pears on 4 plates, arrange the vegetables and red-wine shallots next to them, and season to taste with pepper (M). Cut the venison into serving slices, distribute among the plates, and season to taste with sea salt (Wa). Serve accompanied by the sauce.

Index

Credits

Published originally under the title FENG SHUI UND DIE 5-ELEMENTE-KÜCHE

©2000 by Gräfe und Unzer Verlag GmbH, Munich English translation ©2000 by Silverback Books, Inc.

EDITORS: Ina Schröter, Jennifer Newens
READERS: Linde Wiesner, Vené Franco
TRANSLATOR: Katherine Cofer
LAYOUT AND DESIGN: Claudia Fillmann, Medien-Design; Shanti Nelson
STOCK PHOTOS:
FoodPhotography Eising
ADDITIONAL PHOTOS: Flora Press, p. 10
Giemmegi cucine, p. 22
Hamlyn, p. 21 (Peter Myers)
Jahreis, pp. 25, 29
Jahreszeiten Verlag, pp. 14, 26
SCAN, p. 16
StockFood Eising, pp. 15, 31, 38, 46, 49, 52
Studio R. Schmitz, p. 18, 28
Tielsa—die exclusive Küche, pp. 19, 24, 33

Tony Stone, p. 9 (Gay Bumgarner), p. 11 (David Roth), p. 20 (Simon Rattensby), p. 30 (Roy Botterell), p. 37 (Walter Hodges), p. 43 (Bruce Hands), p. 51 (Ian O'Leary), p. 55 (Ken Scott)
ILLUSTRATIONS: Heidemarie Vignati, p. 23, 41, 42, 48
Martin Scharf, p. 13
TEST KITCHEN: Daniela Bauer, Claudia Bruckmann, Marianne Obermayer, Sabina Träxler, Stefanie von Werz

Printed in Hong Kong through Global Interprint, Santa Rosa, California, USA

ISBN: 1-930603-35-5

Ilse Maria Fahrnow is a doctor specializing in ancient Chinese medicine, homeopathy, and holistic medicine. She practices in Munich.

Jürgen Heinrich Fahrnow is a chef and sommelier. He has trained as a dietician for Chinese medicine and holds seminars on this subject all over the world.

Günther Sator was the first European expert to adapt Feng Shui to the Western lifestyle. He is one of the leading consultants to banks, businesses, and individuals. He is the founder of the Feng Shui Academy in Germany and has written a number of other best-selling books on the subject.

Susie M. and Pete Eising have studios in Munich, Germany, and Kennebunkport, Maine. They studied at the Munich Academy of Photography, where they established their own studio for food photography in 1991.

FOR THIS BOOK:
PHOTOGRAPHY: Martina Görlach
FOOD STYLING: Monika Schuster

COVER PHOTO:
Sea Bass with Wild Rice, page 159